D1766382

Gwasanaeth Llyfrgelloedd Powys Library Service
www.powys.gov.uk/libraries

00540937   917.304

Barcode No. ....   Class No. ....

MACDONELL, A.G.

A visit to America

This book must be returned by the last date stamped above.
Rhaid dychwelyd y llyfr hwn erbyn y dyddiad diwethaf a stampiwyd uchod.

A charge will be made for any lost, damaged or overdue books.
Codir tal os bydd llyfr wedi ei golli neu ei ni weidio neu heb ei ddychwelyd mewn pryd.

The following titles are all in the *Fonthill Complete A. G. Macdonell* Series.
The year indicates when the first edition was published.
See **www.fonthillmedia.com** for details.

Fiction

England, their England (1933)
How Like an Angel   (1934)
Lords and Masters   (1936)
The Autobiography of a Cad   (1939)
Flight From a Lady   (1939)
Crew of the Anaconda (1940)

Short Stories

The Spanish Pistol   (1939)

Non-Fiction

Napoleon and his Marshals   (1934)
A Visit to America   (1935)
My Scotland   (1937)

Crime and Thrillers written under the pseudonym of John Cameron

The Seven Stabs   (1929)
Body Found Stabbed   (1932)

Crime and Thrillers written under the pseudonym of Neil Gordon

The New Gun Runners (1928)
The Factory on the Cliff   (1928)
The Professor's Poison (1928)
The Silent Murders   (1929)
The Big Ben Alibi   (1930)
Murder in Earl's Court (1931)
The Shakespeare Murders   (1933)

A VISIT TO AMERICA

A. G. MACDONELL

FONTHILL

TO MY FRIENDS, GEORGE BRETT JUNIOR, HOYT PERRY, AND
RUSS MACDONALD, ALL OF NEW YORK CITY, WITHOUT WHOSE
TIRELESS ENERGY, UNFAILING KINDNESS, AND UNSTINTED HELP,
THIS VISIT WOULD HAVE BEEN BUT A SHADOW OF ITSELF.

"What is this you bring my America? Is it not something that has been better
told or done before?" WALT WHITMAN.

Fonthill Media Limited
Fonthill Media LLC
www.fonthillmedia.com
office@fonthillmedia.com

First published 1935
This edition published 2014

British Library Cataloguing in Publication Data:
A catalogue record for this book is available from the British Library

Copyright © In Introduction, Fonthill Media 2014

ISBN 978-1-78155-032-8

Typeset in 11pt on 14pt Sabon.
Printed and bound in England.

INTRODUCTION.

Archibald Gordon Macdonell – Archie – was born on 3 November 1895 in Poona, India, the younger son of William Robert Macdonell of Mortlach, a prominent merchant in Bombay, and Alice Elizabeth, daughter of John Forbes White, classical scholar and patron of the arts. It seems likely that Archie was named after Brevet-Colonel A. G. Macdonell, CB, presumably an uncle, who commanded a force that defeated Sultan Muhammed Khan at the fort of Shabkader in the Afghan campaign of 1897.

The family left India in 1896 and Archie was brought up at 'Colcot' in Enfield, Middlesex, and the Macdonell family home of 'Bridgefield', Bridge of Don, Aberdeen. He was educated at Horris Hill preparatory school near Newbury, and Winchester College, where he won a scholarship. Archie left school in 1914, and two years later, he joined the Royal Field Artillery of the 51st Highland Division as a second lieutenant. His experiences fighting on the Western Front were to have a great influence on the rest of his life.

The 51st, known by the Germans as the 'Ladies from Hell' on account of their kilts, were a renowned force, boasting engagements at Beaumont-Hamel, Arras, and Cambrai. But by the time of the 1918 Spring Offensives, the division was war-worn and under strength; it suffered heavily, and Archie Macdonell was invalided back to England, diagnosed with shell shock.

After the war, Macdonell worked with the Friends' Emergency and War Victims Relief Committee, a Quaker mission, on reconstruction in eastern Poland and famine in Russia. Between 1922 and 1927 he was on the headquarters staff of the League of Nations Union, which has prominent mention in Flight from a Lady and Lords and Masters. In the meantime, he stood unsuccessfully as Liberal candidate for Lincoln in the general elections of 1923 and '24. On 31 August 1926, Macdonell married Mona Sabine Mann, daughter of the artist Harrington Mann and his wife Florence Sabine Pasley. They had one daughter, Jennifer. It wasn't a happy marriage, and they divorced in 1937, Mona citing her husband's adultery.

A. G. Macdonell began his career as an author in 1927 writing detective stories, sometimes under the pseudonyms Neil Gordon or John Cameron. He was also highly regarded at this time as a pugnacious and perceptive drama critic; he frequently contributed to the London Mercury, a literary journal founded in 1919 by John Collings Squire, the poet, writer, and journalist, and Archie's close friend.

By 1933 Macdonell had produced nine books, but it was only with the publication in that year of England, Their England that he truly established his reputation as an author. A gentle, affectionate satire of eccentric English customs and society, England, Their England was highly praised and won the prestigious James Tait Black Award in 1933. Macdonell capitalized on this success with another satire, How Like an Angel (1934), which parodied the 'bright young things' and the British legal system. The military history Napoleon and his Marshals (1934) signaled a new direction; although Macdonell thought it poorly rewarded financially, the book was admired by military experts, and it illustrated the range of his abilities. Between 1933 and 1941, A. G. Macdonell produced eleven more books, including the superlative Lords and Masters (1936), which tore into 1930s upper-class hypocrisy in a gripping and prescient thriller, and The Autobiography of a Cad (1939), an hilarious mock-memoir of one Edward Fox-Ingleby, ruthless landowner, unscrupulous politician, and consummate scoundrel.

While many of these works are praised for their teasing exposure of quintessential Englishness, Macdonell delights readers of Visit to America (1934) by satirising Europeans and Americans alike, often with an effortlessly brutal honesty that reveals the absurd and frequently ridiculous eccentricities of all nations, from the Englishman's incessant desire to visit Harlem, the 'lying excuses and side-stepping evasions' that are 'so essentially' European, and the hypocritical relish with which America acknowledges itself as a new country.

The travelogue is based on Macdonell's own visit to America in 1934, by which time he had already enjoyed literary recognition on both sides of the Atlantic. As implied in the opening pages, in which we envisage the author leaning 'in a superior manner' on the rail of the ship, enjoying the perks reserved of those who 'have taken the precaution of travelling first class', Macdonell arrived in America a wealthy celebrity. Accordingly, the book is quick to establish the elevated tone of the distanced observer; one who can partake in the endless cycles of cocktail parties and gentlemen's clubs with the same ease that he may comment on the squalor and dilapidation of broken down warehouses and slums of Baltimore. Yet the voice of the removed traveler is in part misleading, for the carefully paced, whimsical style belies

Macdonell's startlingly acute observations and the piercing wit that drives his savagely humorous depictions of the buildings, parties, transport, churches, and ultimately the people that he encounters.

As Macdonell himself is keen to state throughout, he is not concerned with 'writing about historical events, nor in writing about great public buildings'. Instead, he sought out a rather unusual route through America, passing through Omaha, Nebraska, Montana, and Salt Lake City, as well as the more typical tourist destinations such as New York, San Francisco, and Los Angeles. Macdonell thereby gives readers a unique insight into the ship yards, municipal courtrooms, open plains, and railways of 1930s America, successfully creating a satire that is all the more uniquely amusing and crushingly real, and something that could not be easily experienced elsewhere.

One of the most comically scathing extracts records Macdonell's visit to Chicago, a city he rather disgustedly refers to as 'a disreputable alley-cat that only hopes that no one will pay any attention to it while it slinks from garbage-tin to garbage-tin'. His unflinching attack on America's second city, which he adds, 'seems to give the impression that the drainage system is not what it might be', exemplifies his wonderfully vivid, outrageously amusing, and utterly ruthless style. These cutting descriptions are often offset by recollections of the beauty that Macdonell experienced on the road, such as the magnificence of Michigan Boulevard, the play of light along the Hudson River as the sun descends, and the diversity of colour on the Nebraskan plains. Such observations, rather scarce as they are, provide a distinct contrast to the humorously cruel descriptions that constitute the majority of the travelogue, and frequently serve to render these moments of brutal satire all the more deliciously biting. Although at times the severity of his descriptions seems almost a little too harsh, it is in fact one of the most impressive feats of Visit to America, for Macdonell's uncompromising honesty in no way tarnishes the fluidity of his carefully controlled prose, and each anti-aesthetic detail becomes an essential part of an America alive with energy, enthusiasm, and diversity; ultimately leaving readers with an image of a country that is refreshing in its satirically exposed imperfection.

While states and cities are captured with a precise eye, Macdonell's observations also delve beneath the exteriors of the buildings and transport systems to the politics, racial tensions, religions, and – as expected of a country suffering the Great Depression – the issues of wealth and class that collectively influence the fabric of society. In New York he takes a ride with a Jewish cab driver, who explores with him the inequality between the rich and the poor. In Omaha he spends an evening in the company of an African

American singer, who laments that 'our two races just misunderstand each other', while in Nebraska his meeting with a gaffawing farmer instigates a melancholic reflection on Western politics. Many of these topics are dealt with in a manner that seems wincingly incorrect, or at least alien, to society now, but the picture Macdonell evokes stays undeniably true to America as it stood eighty years ago, and more often than not, people from all walks of life are subjected to the same combination of mildly amused questioning and hard hitting sarcasm.

The overall effect of the memoir is at once flippantly cruel, affectionately teasing, and incredibly honest; a combination that could only be derived through the empathetic intimacy of the most perceptive and compassionate of travelers.

Six years after the publication of Visit to America, in 1940, Macdonell married his second wife, Rose Paul-Schiff, a Viennese whose family was connected with the banking firm of Warburg Schiff. His health had been weak since the First World War, and he died suddenly of heart failure in his Oxford home on 16 January 1941 at the age of 45.

A tall, athletic man with a close-cropped moustache, he was remembered as a complex individual, 'delightful ... but quarrelsome and choleric' by the writer Alec Waugh, who called him the Purple Scot, and by J. B. Morton as, 'A man of conviction, with a quick wit and enthusiasm and ... a sense of compassion for every kind of unhappiness.'

CHAPTER ONE

Approaching Manhattan up by the long-stretching island.

WALT WHITMAN.

The voyage was uneventful. My main impressions of it were the width of the Atlantic, which I had never before crossed, the number of references made by my fellow passengers to the salutary effect of sea-air upon the human constitution, and the benevolent expression upon the face of President Harding, whose portrait presided, like a Patron Saint, over most of our activities. It is true, now that I come to look back upon it, that few, if any, Americans on the ship referred to Mr. Harding in conversation as a Saint, or seemed at all pleased to be sailing under his Patronage. But perhaps they were political opponents, and therefore biased against the good man. At any rate they were unanimous, for some reason which I could not fathom, in the opinion that no ship connected in any way with President Harding was likely to run out of oil.

On the morning of the seventh day the first incident occurred since the evening at Cobh (*née* Queenstown), when dainty Irish colleens had tried to sell us genuine hand-made peasant lace from Manchester, and broths of boys had offered us unique bargains (mass-produced) in shillelaghs. We saw land. Long Island appeared on the horizon.

A few hours later we arrived at Quarantine and halted for the Medical Examination. It was a long business, but it incommoded us not a whit. For the Hygienic Theory of the United States appears to be based on a remarkable notion. Anyone who can afford to buy a first-class ticket is automatically presumed to be free from all contagious infection. A doctor coming from a campaign against bubonic plague in Turkey, a medical missionary from the yellow fever districts of Central Africa, an explorer from the typhus-infested villages of Turkestan, all these are exempt from medical inspection if they have taken the precaution of travelling first class. But let a man be as free from germs as an iceberg, and let him scrub himself in antiseptics three times a day, and let him travel in the steerage class, and by Heavens! he will learn that Quarantine is no idle word.

For at least an hour we leant in a superior manner on the rail, while our poorer fellow passengers were presumed to be suffering from the deadliest and most baffling diseases known to, or unknown by, medical science, and as we leant we affirmed and re-affirmed and stated frankly and repeated with the utmost emphasis at our command, to each and all our charming American friends on board, that the Skyline of Manhattan not only came up to, but far exceeded our wildest, our most hallucinatory we groped frantically for bigger, taller words expectations.

As the liner steamed slowly up the Hudson, the stream of expert pointers-out grew thicker and thicker, and better and better informed. "The one on the left, Mr. Macdonell, is the Woolworth Building; next to it is the Chrysler Building, and beyond the Chrysler is the Empire State. But the building which you can't see is Number One, Broadway, the office of the Standard Oil Company."

After I had duly pigeonholed this information, the next one would reverse the order of the buildings, and add that I couldn't see Number One, Broadway, the office of the Cunard Company, and then a third would substitute the R.C.A. for Woolworth, and the Irving Trust for the Empire State, and add that Number One, Broadway, was the office of Messrs, J. P. Morgan. But all were agreed on one point, the invisibility of that mysterious building. (I never discovered whether they were right or not, but I should imagine that they were not.)

As we advanced closer and closer, the effect of the Skyline was somewhat counter-balanced by the sinking feeling induced by the nearness of the Customs Examination. In Europe we hear more about the horrors of the latter even than about the magnificence of the former. Indeed, we have long grown accustomed to travellers tales in our Club of the brutal Irish Inspectors who, as soon as they hear an English accent on the Quay, either scatter white waistcoats in the dust what time they mutter "Robert Emmet ... Wolfe Tone ... Charles Stewart Parnell," in a savage undertone, and fling shirts and ties about to the tune of the "Shan Van Voght," or else stand for hours in a trance, murmuring verses from Yeats "The Countess Cathleen," and refusing to undertake so mundane a task as the inspection of the baggage.

But it appears either that things have changed since our fellow Clubmen crossed the Atlantic under sail, or else that they are confusing their recollections of the New York Customs with those of the spirited scenes at the capture of the Lahore Gate at Delhi, during the Indian Mutiny of 1857. However that may be, I landed with some nervousness, for the Quay was very dusty and I knew that my evening waistcoats were very white. But within half an hour I had been passed through with perfect politeness and total absence of fuss.

A friend met me, threw me into a taxi, and within forty minutes of setting foot on American soil, I was at my first party.

I had been assured that it would only be a small party, so that I should not be unduly confused at meeting too many total strangers all at once, and I was all the more grateful for this kindly consideration when I was shot out of the taxi into the middle of a mere two hundred people, of whom one hundred and ninety-seven were total strangers. Each one of them asked me how long I had been in America, and to each I replied, forty-five minutes, forty-six and a half minutes, forty-nine minutes, and so on, as time went on and my visit lasted longer and longer. At about eight P.M., when I had shaken hands with about a hundred and fifty people, I began to feel more grateful than ever that it was only a small party. Luckily for me it turned out to be not only a small party but an early one. About thirty of us went on to dinner at the Plaza Hotel and after a few hours dancing I got home to my hotel at about four A.M.

Next morning I awoke at about eight o clock and began to revolve plans for sight-seeing. It was clear that the first week or two in such a staggering colossus of a place as New York ought to be spent very slowly. It is the sign of an inexperienced traveller to race round from sight to sight, guide-book in one hand and pencil in the other, pockets bulging with note-books and picture postcards, and with each hour of the day mapped out by stop-watch. The only way to absorb any sort of atmosphere is to loaf round in a very leisurely fashion, or, better still, to sit down and wait for the atmosphere to come for absorption. I decided, therefore, to lie in bed every morning until about 9.30 studying the daily newspapers, and to sally out for a gentle stroll at about eleven. Luncheon would occupy the hours between one and three P.M., and for the rest of the day a bench in Central Park, or perhaps in Battery Park, would provide an admirable base for observation, reflection, and the general absorption of atmosphere.

This plan of campaign having been sketched out, and the hour being by now 8.30 A.M., I was about to go to sleep again when my bedside telephone rang, and from that instant until I steamed out of New York Harbour several months later, I do not suppose that I had an aggregate period of leisure of more than one hour and forty minutes altogether. The nearest I ever got to a bench in Central Park was on a morning in December when I ran madly across the Park to a luncheon engagement which I had endeavoured to keep in East Eighty-first Street when I ought to have been keeping it in West Eighty-first Street; and I once had three minutes in Battery Park between two appointments. As for gentle strolls, I managed to bring off about half a dozen all told, but as they were usually on the way back from parties at about six A.M. I was seldom in a state of sufficient mental alertness to take notes or to jot down impressions.

From the moment that my telephone-bell rang on that first morning, I was caught up in the whizzing, whirling, skyrocketing, Rush of life in New York. There was never time for anything except a frantic leap into a taxi, and a furious drive to the next engagement. Sometimes when traffic was busy and I was in an exceptionally violent hurry, I used to run from engagement to engagement in order to arrive more quickly than was possible by taxi, and I used to notice that out of the crowds of pedestrians through whom I dodged and side-stepped, about fifteen per cent were also running and eighty-five per cent were walking as quickly as they could. Everyone was caught up in the Rush. At first I was enormously impressed by the scurrying masses and their zeal to be at something or other, and it was not until much later that I began to discover one or two peculiar features of the New Yorker's haste to transport himself, whether horizontally or vertically, from one spot to another.

For instance, after accompanying many charming New York friends in swift dashes hither and thither through their city, I began to notice that the moment they reached their destination all the hurry stopped. They would save three minutes on the journey and then waste twenty in doing nothing in particular. One of the favourite topics of conversation, especially Downtown, is the prime necessity of getting down to business at once because of the incredibly short length of time at the disposal of the conversationalists. Taxis and legs save minutes that minds do not seem to know what to do with. Even on that very first morning I ought to have suspected something of this, for the man who telephoned to me at the ungodly hour of 8.30 devoted the first fourteen minutes of his call to explanations of, and apologies for, his inability to call me up any later in the day. He was too busy, he said. And naturally I was too civil to point out that he would have got the same telephonic results, achieved the same volume of business, saved several dimes on his telephone account, and allowed me another fourteen minutes rest, if he had called up at 8.44 A.M. In any case I doubt if he would have believed me. It takes unpractical literary folk to see things like that.

The stock explanation of this perpetual physical activity of the New Yorker is, of course, the Air, which is generally conceded to be just like champagne by a nation that probably knows less about champagne, owing to long years of inexperience, than almost any other nation in the world. But if that be the true explanation surely the Air ought to stimulate him to perpetual mental activity as well. However, that is a speculation that not only is outside the scope of this work, but is verging on dangerous ground.

After the first fourteen minutes of that telephone-call, my business-friend came down to the matter in hand, and by nine o clock, or it may have been a few minutes after, had invited me to a party and I had gratefully accepted.

The telephone rang fairly continuously all morning, and during the next four days I went to sixteen cocktail parties, four dinner parties, four supper parties, and four dances. On the fifth day I went to bed.

But cocktail parties were not the only form of hospitality into which I was thrown. There was, for instance, the Businessman's luncheon. This is a most impressive function. It begins, as a rule, sharp at one P.M. It concludes sharp at two P.M. Nothing is drunk except iced water and coffee, and when it is over the iron-jawed hustlers return to their offices and telephone to San Francisco or New Orleans or somewhere, It is an amazing contrast to the corresponding entertainment in England which begins about 12.45, and goes on till about three, to the somnolent accompaniment of sherry, tankards of beer, and liqueur brandies.

But although during those first weeks of wild helter-skelter it was very difficult to form any sort of impression about New York, its flora and fauna for it was only rarely that I was allowed to rise to the surface for a moment's breath before being ruthlessly submerged by another flood of kindness nevertheless I did manage to pick up some useful bits of learning. One thing, for example, I learnt, and that was the injustice that is done to visiting British authors by the people of New York. At every party I went to, at least six people said to me, "Why do British authors come over here for a fortnight and then go home and write an unkind book about us?"

At first I could make no reply except a giggle or some sort of strangled noise of deprecation and apology at the back of my throat. After all it is not an easy question to answer until you know the truth and then it becomes perfectly simple. This is the truth. British authors visit the United States with the full intention of staying five or six months, of studying sociological, political, industrial, and economic conditions, of talking earnestly to men and women in all walks of life, of visiting every State in the Union, and, in fact, of making a real job of it. Then, their investigations completed, their note-books bulging with notes, and their memories with impressions, they propose to return to Europe and compile a book that shall be a classic of sympathetic comment and impartial analysis. That is their intention, and not even the most bigoted adherent of the international theories of Big Bill Thompson could find fault with it. But what happens? The author comes bowling ashore at the Cunard quay, full of robust health, with clear eye and upright carriage. Three weeks later he sneaks back on board, trembling, bloodshot, jumping at the slightest sound, rapidly greying round the temples and thinning on top, peering furtively about him, hoarse, terrified. He is suffering from lack of sleep, incipient delirium tremens, loss of appetite, surfeit of oysters, gout, and cirrhosis of the liver. On the voyage home he stays locked in his cabin for fear that his so-called friends in New York may have acquaintances on the ship to whom they may have recommended him for entertainment. He tries to avert the delirium tremens by abjuring all alcohol on the voyage, and arrives home in a fearful rage induced by stuffy air in the cabin, liver, lack of exercise, and the sudden cutting-off of stimulant. In a blind fury he sits down at his desk and writes 70,000 words of pure poison about the authors of his malaise. Thus have the kindly citizens of the United States defeated their own object. Intent upon giving a merry time to a stranger, and thereby giving him also a good impression of themselves, they reduce him from a well-intentioned Innocent Abroad to a surly and cantankerous wreck, and then are pained and surprised when the resulting travel-book arrives, sizzling with sulphur and brimstone, from the printing-presses.

Another discovery I made during this wild round of gaiety was the list of subjects on which Americans do not like being laughed at, however gentle and good-humoured the laughter. It is a list which every stranger in a strange land has to compile at the earliest possible moment if he is to avoid giving offence and being ignominiously kicked out, and it is a list which every country possesses. The French have the shortest, and at the same time the largest. It consists of one word, France. The English, as I have pointed out elsewhere, have two patches of consecrated ground, the Team Spirit at Cricket, and Admiral Lord Nelson. The Italians, on the contrary, have a list as long as your arm, ranging from ice-cream to Caporetto. In America, at any rate north of the Mason and Dixon Line, there is only one real Taboo for the foreigner and, strangely enough, it is one of the things that Americans themselves take a painful, an almost morbid, pleasure in talking about. But the foreigner must keep off it. He may laugh at his hosts for anything else in the world — and they, being happy and good-natured people, will laugh gaily with him — but on this subject, alone of all subjects, he must preserve the most incommunicable of silences, not only of word and of laughter, but also of gesture whether of hand, shoulder, or eyebrow. Otherwise he will be utterly damned to all eternity, and will miss all the loveliness, all the strangeness, all the fantastic surprises, of this lovely, strange, fantastic, and surprising continent.

Even now, writing in the safe security of England, behind the yawning guns of the Royal British Navy, three thousand miles from New York City, I am nervously diffident of even writing down the fearful secret. Wild horses, those legendary draggers of secrets, would not drag it from me in plain word of mouth. If is quite dangerous enough to commit it to paper.

But the truth of the matter is, and I record it with misgiving, reluctance, and a sense of imminent calamity, that the American does not like strangers to say that America is a new country. He himself will say it, over and over again, but it is as much as your life is worth to say it yourself. It is risky even to agree with him when he says it. In fact, it is safer either to say nothing at all in answer to him, or to confine yourself to a muttered reference to Thorfinn Karlsefne or Leif Ericsson.

It is a peculiar business, the American attitude to Antiquity. Of all the citizens of the world there is none so alive as the American to the value of modernity, so fertile in experiment, so feverish in the search for something new. There is nothing from Architecture to Contract Bridge, from the Immortality of the Soul to the Ventilation of Railroad-Cars, from Golf to God, that he does not pounce upon and examine critically to see if it cannot be improved. And then, having pulled it to pieces, mastered its fundamental theory, and re-assembled it in a novel and efficient design, he laments bitterly because it is not old. The one great quality which America has brought to civilization, is the very quality that Americans wring their hands over. Scotland does not admit the superiority of England because the clans were barbarous cattle-thieves when Alcuin was Archbishop of York and the friend of Charlemagne, nor do the English regard themselves as a lower order of humanity than the Italians because the English were facing the rigours of their climate in a coating of woad when Virgil was riding with Horace down the Appian Way. But the American has got this notion into his head and nothing will expel it, and he takes a morbid delight in trotting it out in public and wringing his hands over it. He has created a bogey and is cowed by it. But woe betide the foreigner who so much as hints at the existence of the bogey. A perfect example of this American indecision whether to worship a thing because it is New, or to worship it because it is Old, is to be found in the town-planning and street-naming of New York City.

It is an important boast of the citizen of Manhattan that his streets possess the simplest, the most logical, the most practical system of identification in the world. The avenues run north and south and are numbered from One to Thirteen; the streets run east and west and are numbered from One to One Million as the case may be. The corners are all right-angles, the intervals between the streets identical. Therefore, cries the New Yorker raising his voice a little in order to be audible above the sound of a passing elevated train, a simple calculation gives you the exact distance which has to be traversed on any journey between two known points, and furthermore the mere mention of an address at once establishes the exact position of that particular spot on the island. Complicated explanations are unnecessary. How much simpler than elaborate postal districts such as plague the Londoner! How much simpler than the *arrondissements* of Paris! To this cry of triumph is often added a gentle suggestion that such efficiency, such practical modernity, is characteristic of the nation which long ago swept away the ridiculous coinage of England and substituted the metric dollar.

Both claims are beautifully absurd. The American, a sentimentalist to the core, clings passionately to the yard, the furlong, and the mile; he sells his wheat by the bushel and his cotton by the bale. There is no reckoning in kilo-bales on the Carolinian plantations, or kilo-bushels on the long plains of Nebraska. The tough placer-miner of the Northwest reckons his gold-dust by the ounce, and that not even the simple ounce of his brother, the lead-miner of Missouri. Troy weight, with its minims and pennyweights, is the reckoning for the gold-miner in the logical New World, as in the unpractical Old.

And so it is in Manhattan, The avenues run north and south and are numbered from One to Thirteen. But what does the poor stranger do when, leaving Third Avenue and making for Fourth Avenue, he suddenly finds himself in Lexington Avenue? And what happens to his confidence in his bump of locality when he strolls along Eleventh, finds himself suddenly in Thirteenth, goes a little further in the same direction and presto! he is in Twelfth? It is just the same with the streets. The numbers run with beautiful regularity, and the rectangles are laid out with perfect symmetry, down from the hundreds into the eighties and the forties, and then suddenly Broadway appears, wandering in a most sloppy way at a slant across the island, and curling about at random hither and thither in the most unprofessional style. Affairs get worse still as we go south. After First Street, Manhattan fairly plunges into an orgy of sentiment. Old heroes are commemorated and pastoral memories revived. Here once was the Bowling Green on which the grave burgesses unbent for an hour in solemn dignity. There ran the Wall, and beyond it, long ago, stood a Pine and a Cedar. They must have been patriarchs among trees to have resisted so bravely the iniquity of oblivion. The Rose flowered inside the Wall, and the Mulberry, and there was once an Orchard. There are no shepherdesses now in Gramercy Park and it is many a year since Greene was green, but the lovely old names are there, each with its memory of a past that stretches back a long while before some standardizing genius hit upon the notion of the numbered street and the rectangular corner and the uniform block. That southern end of Manhattan is a mass of history. Frankfort and Hanover streets are surely echoes of those German mercenaries whom England bought and unleashed upon her own kinsmen, Nassau and Dutch must be survivals from New Amsterdam, and Bowery was once spelt Bouwerie. In Battery Park there is the statue of Verrazano, that bold Florentine, who came sailing up the

Hudson River in 1525, the year of the Battle of Pavia when all was lost to the Fortune of France, save Honour and the life of King Francis. In the graveyard of the Church of the Trinity, in Broadway opposite the end of Wall Street is buried James Lawrence, the captain of the famous frigate *Chesapeake*, and near by is the grave of an English captain of the Ninth Regiment of Infantry, and beyond him are the "Late Agent of His Britannick Majesty's Packets" and William Bradford, printer, "born in Leicestershire in Old England in 1660, for 50 years printer to This Government."

I spent a long time in the graveyard of the Church of the Trinity, looking at the tombstones and trying to decipher the inscriptions. And then it suddenly struck me that it was a very extraordinary thing that there should be any difficulty about deciphering the inscriptions. After all, here was an authentic piece of that Antiquity which the Americans so passionately long for. Here, in the Trinity churchyard, lie men who took part in the making of the United States. (The parish dates from 1697.) But the stones are neglected and the inscriptions are often almost illegible, and an atmosphere of decay broods over the scene. It is as if a compromise has been arranged between the rival forces of Antiquity and Modernity. The Modern Spirit allows the church and its burial ground to remain in the heart of the financial district where site-values must be about a million dollars a square inch, while in return the Spirit of Antiquity makes the concession that the historical relics of America's past shall be allowed to rot away to dust.

CHAPTER TWO

Give me faces and streets — give me those phantoms
    incessant and endless along the trottoirs!
Give me interminable eyes — give me women — give me
    comrades and lovers by the thousand!
Let me see new ones every day — let me hold new ones by
    the hand every day!
Give me such shows — give me the streets of Manhattan!

WALT WHITMAN.

In spite of the Rush, and the incessant telephone-calls, and the hospitality, it does occasionally happen to the visitor in New York that his tireless hosts make a miscalculation in their plans for his entertainment. Nine times out of ten the error takes the form of providing six parties for the same hour on the same day. The tenth time — and how rarely does it seem to come along — is when they leave a whole hour unoccupied by meal, drink, dance, or personally conducted tour. This tenth time, this blessed blank, did happen to me once or twice during the four or five weeks I spent in the City, and I was able to carry out a small fraction of my original, illusory programme and stroll at leisure through the streets and watch the crowds hurrying past. But although it is difficult to stroll at leisure through the streets of New York, it is fifty times more difficult to write about it.

For what is there to say about New York that has not been said a thousand times before? Description may run into volumes or may be crystallized into a single phrase, as that great American crystallized it when he called it Baghdad-on-the-Subway. There was never a more perfect description of a town. Later American wits have followed in O. Henry's path and have called Los Angeles "Twelve Suburbs in Search of a City," and Waco, that queer Texan town with its single skyscraper amid the interminable ranges, "A Totem-Pole Completely Surrounded by Baptists," but they have never come within miles of the profundity and wisdom of Baghdad-on-the-Subway. There you have New York. The splendour and the luxury and the wealth of the East live again in this city of the West. No oriental palace could be more fantastic than the Chrysler Building which begins as a concrete sky scraper, develops into a specimen of loathsome fret work in metal, and tapers off into a comic needle like the horn of a narwhal that is suffering from elephantiasis. Caliphs as wealthy as Haroun drive about the streets. Jewels as rare as the Timur ruby are on sale in the bazaars.

All the world meets in the New Baghdad. In an hour's walk you can see men of China and Japan, of Africa and the primeval jungle, of the Hebrews, that ancient race, of Europe and of Siberia, of the Arctic Circle and of the hot damp swamps of the Equator. The caravans of the Five Continents converge on the New Baghdad, as they used to on the old. The merchants and the money-lenders of the world listen to every faint ripple of sound in the markets that cluster where the old city wall once stood, and the story of Ali Baba and the forty thieves is exactly repeated when two oil-kings join in the deadly combat of price-cutting competition. One or other of them dies a financial death when oil falls.

Mosques and minarets and cupolas are dotted over the island that lies, as Mesopotamia lies, between the two rivers, and the merchant-princes have scattered over the city, with a lavish prodigality, their monuments to their own glory. Generally their monuments are buildings, in which men and women may toil at ledgers and typewriters nearer to God than ever men and women toiled before, and sometimes they are libraries or collections of art treasures that have been won in many a swift invasion into older and more effete countries.

And all the time there is the Subway, roaring, tearing, rattling, swiftly, noisily, dirtily, underneath the palaces of the Latterday Caliphs. There is all the splendour of the East on Park Avenue, and all the squalor of the East below the bridges in Brooklyn. For every Baghdad palace there is a Manhattan palace and for every Baghdad beggar there is a Manhattan beggar. Splendour here, and poverty there. That is New York. Step for one moment off the great thoroughfare, and the slums are yelling round you. It is only a few yards from the swishing stream of the great automobiles to the howl of the elevated railway and the whine of the street-cars. Stand on one of the great thoroughfares, Broadway for instance, which shares the fame of Piccadilly, the Champs Elysées, Unter den Linden, and the Appian Way and watch the rich go past. Then stroll down the street till you come to a grating in the side walk and pause there. In a moment you will hear a roaring sound and feel a rush of disturbed air. The sidewalk will tremble and then the sound will die away. That is the noise of a train in the Subway. You have heard the poor go past. Rattling, swaying, jolting, jammed so tightly against one another that strap-hanging is unnecessary because it is impossible to fall, smelling, dirty, harassed, the poor go riding in the Subway. Nobody cares where they go or what they do. For a nickel the Subway is open to all. Stay there a minute or a month — nobody cares. A nickel has bought the Freedom of Sub-New York and you may live there or die there, whichever you please, and no single fellow human being will do anything more to you than jostle you out of the way. He will not even look at you as he jostles. He would not even look at you as he tripped over your dead body. There are very few indicators in the big stations to guide the inexperienced traveller to his correct platform because nobody cares two straws whether the inexperienced traveller gets to his correct platform or not.

The Caliphs never see the poor. The poor would catch a glimpse of the Caliphs if they had time to wait for a few hours at a street-corner and could recognize a Caliph when they saw one. But the poor are too busy, rushing hither and thither, either on their own obscure and humble little errands which do not really need such haste, or upon the tremendous errands of the Caliphs themselves, and these require most peremptorily all the haste in the world. So New Baghdad, the real New Baghdad, never meets its own Subway. It only vaguely knows that it exists, somewhere deep down in the earth, out of sight, and very unimportant. For the Latterday Caliph does not even wander the streets at night, like Haroun or Florizel, in search of the quaint, the bizarre, the picturesque. He has read too many stories in the newspapers (which he probably owns) of men who went out walking and were battered with sandbags or perforated by sub-machine-gun bullets for their trouble.

On the first occasion when my hosts left a mysterious gap in the schedule, I spent it, naturally, gaping up at the skyscrapers. But this is no place to talk about skyscrapers. They have been spoken of before. In England, they are usually described as tall but vulgar, and sometimes as vulgar but tall, and intending travellers are advised to have their hearts tested before ascending to the top of the highest ones. Needless to say, like almost all English theories about America, these ideas are quite wrong except the idea that they are tall. One or two of the earlier skyscrapers are over-ornamented and ugly. But the newer ones, with their severe, clean lines, are extraordinarily beautiful. After dark they turn Manhattan from a scramble of money-makers into a fantastical city of magic with squares of orange light that glow in the sky only an inch or two below Arcturus, and turn the dullest street into a fairy canyon, while in the daytime the glass and the glittering concrete, untarnished by grime in a smokeless town, make a far more brilliant decoration than any colour in the streets. For the streets themselves are drab in comparison, say, with the streets of London. The London buses, like crawling scarlet scarabs, brighten every yard of the main roads. The private automobiles are often sensationally painted. Telephone-boxes are gaily tricked out, and the scarlet pillar-boxes are like round, solid, symbols of John Bull himself. (It is one of John Bull's gnawing miseries that his favourite colour, the scarlet with which he splashes his streets, his stamps, and his Empire upon the map, is the very same as the scarlet of the Revolutionary miscreants of Moscow.) But in New York there are few buses, except a quaint and wobbly service of ancient green contrivances which ply up and down Fifth Avenue, beginning in Washington Square and fading away into nothingness, for all I know into complete dissolution, in the neighbourhood of West 150th Street. A small town in Connemara, Ireland, would turn up its nose at these veterans. The nearest approach to them that I have ever seen was a horse-drawn street-car in Kovno, Capital of Lithuania. It is left to the taxi-cabs to provide the colour in the streets of New York. The private cars (called automobiles for short) are almost always darkest blue or black or a rather dull brown. It is the rarest thing in the world to see a sensational pale green racer, or a stately all-silver limousine. But the fleets of taxis somewhat redeem the drabness. One fleet consists of bright yellow cabs, each one labelled in large letters on each side, "Yellow Taxi." This label is a remarkable piece of thoughtfulness on the part of the owners, for it can only be intended to enliven the dull lives of the Colour-Blind, who would not otherwise know that these taxis are yellow. No one can believe for a minute that the practical American would waste so much time, space, and good black paint in stating such an exceptionally obvious fact, if there was not some altruistic motive behind it. (It is a little more difficult to detect the altruistic motive which has inspired the notice "To the Lower Level" above a yawning abyss of descending stairs in the Grand Central Station. However colour blind a man is, he surely could not fail to detect that stairs going downwards will probably lead to a place on a lower level.)

A second fleet of taxis is painted silver and equipped with radio loud-speakers. When I landed in New York, it was impossible to hire a radio-taxi at all. The reason for this was very singular. It appears that the climax of the baseball season is a match between the champion clubs of the two baseball Leagues. The match consists of a series of games which is continued until one or the other of the two teams has scored four victories, and is called the World Series. Why it should be called the World Series is not very clear. So far as I know, baseball is played to any marked extent only in the United States and in Japan, which cannot cover as much between them as one-tenth of the surface of the world. However, let it pass. There is that hotel in Paris called L'Hotel de 1'Univers et du Portugal, and in London there is a journal for stamp-collectors called "*The World-wide Philatelist*, with which is incorporated *The Kensington Philatelist*" We are all tarred with the same megalomaniac feather.

The World Series on this occasion was to be played between the Detroit Tigers and the New York Giants. Everything was set for it. Businessmen from all over the United States discovered that the fate and fortunes of their corporations depended upon an immediate visit to New York. Board meetings were arranged by the thousand in the neighbourhood of Wall Street. The ground floors of the hotels were crammed with middle-aged gentlemen demonstrating to one another with umbrellas exactly how such-and-such a pitcher could easily be dealt with, and with other middle-aged gentlemen, demonstrating how impossible it was for any batter to hit the devastating pitching of so-and-so. Indeed during these wild days it was practically impossible to get from one side to the other of a hotel-lounge without getting at least one crack in the eye or on the shin bone. And then a truly fearful catastrophe occurred. It was to the tired businessman who had struggled to New York for his board-meeting, the equivalent of the San Francisco earthquake and the Chicago fire. It destroyed his faith never perhaps, overwhelmingly strong in the Divine Guidance of mortal affairs. For a young gentleman named Dizzy Dean, assisted by his brother Daffy, scored an incredible number of victories for the St. Louis Cardinals by his superb pitching, a miserable and obscure team called the Brooklyn Dodgers defeated the New York Giants twice in one week, and bim! The Giants were out, and the Cardinals were in, and the World Series was abducted from New York and deposited overnight in Detroit and St. Louis. Dispirited bands of company directors found that they had no alternative but to attend their board-meetings and then go sulkily home. The crowds in the hotels called sadly for their checks, declared a few dividends, or passed them as the case may be, and returned to such places as Baltimore, Buffalo, Cleveland and Pittsburgh.

Now at last we come to the reason why the taxi- drivers of the Radio fleet were out of circulation during a whole week. Each driver parked his cab at the side of the street, lay down at full length in the back, switched on his radio and listened to the broadcast description of the baseball games.

Although I knew only so much about baseball as can be learned from the newspapers and a very occasional match between a visiting American battleship and the "London Americans," I soon gathered that the elder Mr. Dean has a pretty wit and a nice sense of showmanship, besides being the greatest pitcher since the days of the great Christy Mathewson. It was his genial habit, during the World Series, to march into the dressing-room of the Detroit Tigers and explain to each one of his baffled and indignant opponents exactly how he proposed to deal with them in the forthcoming encounter. I never could quite fathom why someone of the tigrine camp did not sock him on the jaw, but apparently no one ever did. On the other hand Mr. Dean's prose style was distinctly a grade or two below his pitching. This is a sample of it, and I cannot help feeling that it runs to vigour and crisp energy rather than to musical cadences. Asked by a reporter when a slight injury to his head would be sufficiently healed to allow him to pitch again. Dizzy replied: "I would be tickled to death to pitch to-morrow's game. I think I would have my stuff to-morrow, and probably would shut the Detroit Tigers out, because after pitching to-day without my stuff, and they didn't know I didn't have my stuff, I could go out there to-morrow and shut the boys out. I think that if they pitched me the whole four days I would win all four of them." Mr. Dean ultimately found his stuff and pitched the Cardinals into victory in the final game of the Series, and 1,498 correspondents wrote to the *Evening Sun* of Baltimore enclosing a parody of Kipling on the refrain "You're a better man than I am, Dizzy Dean." The following week, a town in Florida called Bradenton changed its name to Deanville.

* * *

During this part of my visit to the United States I was greatly moved by the courtesy and tact of all those citizens who gallantly suppressed visible emotion when I explained that a single cricket-match between England and Australia had been known to last for eight whole days, and that spectators have, on occasion, dislocated their jaws with a yawn.

* * *

But although I missed the great baseball series, I was in time for the football season, and at the earliest possible date I went to see a football game. My knowledge of this pastime had, up to this period, been exclusively drawn from the short stories about it in the *Saturday Evening Post*. The main point of the game, so far as I could gather from these stories, was that each College had its deadly rival College, and that at the end of each season the star quarter-back of one team invariably married the beautiful daughter of the hard-faced Coach of the other. In the last paragraph the star and the daughter fell into a sort of flying tackle, while the Coach sobbed once or twice, convulsively, over the happy pair. The two Colleges, I could only infer, lived on the happiest

23

basis of good-fellowship for several months after this, until the approach of the next football season recalled them to bitterest enmity once more with the knowledge that the new star quarter-back was snooping around after the hard-faced Coach's second daughter. That, roughly speaking, was the essence of football as I had grasped it. Obviously it was my duty to check this impression by a visit to the actual scene.

A party of young ladies and gentlemen of my acquaintance had promised to take me to Princeton to watch the lads of that University competing with the lads of Williams, a similar institution, and they arranged to call for me at my hotel at 11 A.M. on the Saturday of the game, and drive me to Princeton. The first intimation I had of their arrival was at 10.45, when the hall-porter asked me politely whether I knew that some guests were down in the cocktail-bar, drinking whisky and charging it to my room-number. I fled downstairs just in time to keep the score below five dollars, and the drive began. We bowled along the Holland Tunnel and came out, on the New Jersey side, on to the most magnificent and awe-inspiring road I have ever seen. For miles and miles it is lifted clean above the ground on a great ramp of concrete and iron, and there is room for at least six lines of traffic. The moment we were on it, my young host put his foot down on the accelerator pedal and kept it there till we reached Princeton. The pace was fast but not dizzy. I found this almost everywhere I went in the United States, with one notable exception to be described hereafter. The power of the American automobiles is, comparatively speaking, standardized, so that almost all can do seventy-five miles an hour and few can go faster and fewer still have to go more slowly, so that there is not nearly so much passing and re-passing, cutting-in and cutting-out, as there is in Europe. Cars are more inclined to take station, like a warship on manoeuvres, and stay there.

Once off the ramp, you are fairly in the State of New Jersey. It is a flat, dismal country, looking as if an army had passed that way and was even now entrenching against an enemy twenty miles further on. It reminded me of the back-areas in France and Flanders. The fields were desolate. No plough had been there and no human beings walked there. Weeds and nettles and tall, rank grasses quivered forlornly in the faint breeze. Here and there a ruined brick house, or a cluster of old wooden shacks, rotting, crumbling, moss- covered, were a reminder that at one time men had passed this way and lingered awhile before hastening from a solitude that was made the more intolerable by the nearness of a vast city. Sometimes the nettles were clambering over a heap of rusty tins and a bramble bush sprouted through the chassis of a motor car that was standing on its nose in an ancient ditch. This solitude stretches away for miles and miles to the right and left of the road until it reaches the horizons with their ghostly silhouettes of factory chimneys and of long iron bridges, hideous at short range but, seen across the russety-green of the fields, far away, as lovely as dew on a spider's web on a September morning. Sometimes a line of oil-tanks, poised upon steel tripods, marched across the flatlands looking like the Martians of H. G. Wells story.

It was a blessed relief when we left the desolation and ran into the more homely atmosphere of gasoline stations and advertisements for Coca Cola.

The outline of Princeton, on its wooded hill, is very beautiful, but there is less beauty about the faked-Tudor architecture and interior decoration of some of the college buildings. One of the fraternity houses looks more like the England of Queen Elizabeth's day than many a gasoline station on the English roads. But there was no time for the consideration of aesthetics.

Princeton was to play football against Williams, and the Stadium was the magnet. After a few drinks of neat rye whisky to keep out the icy wind, therefore, we repaired to our seats. Truly the Americans are a hardy race. There has been a considerable advance in the standards of comfort in arenas, amphitheatres, and theatres since the ancient Greeks sat huddled upon bare stones at Epidaurus, or the Sicilians at Taormina, but the Americans will have none of it. What was good enough for the Athenian is good enough for him, even though the winds of New Jersey in November are somewhat cooler than the breezes of the Isles of Greece, gilded as they are with eternal summer.

The seats in the Palmer Stadium are just slabs of concrete, and if you do not like them the remedy is entirely in your own hands. There is no compulsion on you to stay. The exits are clearly marked and someone else will be glad of the space you have vacated. We wrapped ourselves in rugs, loosened slightly the tops of our whisky bottles to ensure a freely moving and prompt service, and lowered ourselves, some with enthusiasm, and some with reluctance, and myself with active distaste, on to the icy slabs. A pale, wan sun peered over the rim of the Stadium, and the wind wailed drearily from the direction of the Arctic Circle. The entertainment was due to begin.

First of all came the rival brass-bands, marching, blowing and banging with immense energy, and after them followed twelve beautiful young gentlemen in white shirts and white flannel trousers, each armed with a gaily coloured megaphone. They took station in a line at about fifteen yards intervals, between the field of play and the crowd, and facing the crowd, six on one side of the ground and six on the other. Then the six facing us began to behave in a most extraordinary way. Moving in perfect unison they faced east and slapped their knees, and then they faced west and slapped their knees. They shook their fists now hither, now thither. They waved their arms like men on a raft in mid-ocean who are attempting to attract the attention of passing ships.

25

Finally they worked themselves up into an ecstasy of excitement, flinging their bodies about like demented dervishes, or the High-Priests of some weird religion who are approaching the climax of a ritual, the human sacrifice, for instance, or the self-immolation of the youngest and strongest of the tribe for the greater glory of the tribe, until at last they brought their strange incantations to an end by leaping high into the air and uttering a great cry. Then they sat down on their megaphones. In the meanwhile, the six rivals on the other side of the ground had begun to do their stuff, and were obtaining much more gratifying results than our champions. For the serried ranks of the members of the Williams tribe, or perhaps I should say students and alumni, accepted their six young men as joint-conductors, as it were, of a human orchestra, and they roared savagely in time to the leaps and gesticulations. An almost frightening din came echoing across the Stadium. I enquired why the supporters of Princeton did not do the same. Is it, I asked, owing to the superior gentlemanliness of Princeton students and alumni, that they refrain from competing in noise with the lads from Williams? Is there a tradition of good manners that descends from the days when Nassau Hall was being built in memory, for some reason, of Dutch King William III? Far from it, my hosts replied. The Princeton lads were shouting as loudly as any. But owing to a curious acoustical quality in the Stadium, they went on to explain, it is only possible to hear the noise of the opposition. And after that long explanation it appeared that their throats had gone a bit dry, for they produced a whisky bottle and passed it backwards and forwards a good deal.

Then the teams came out. The Princeton team consisted of about fifty young men, Williams of about thirty, but my expectation of seeing the grand, if some what one-sided, muddle of about eighty husky youths all playing together, was sadly disappointed. Only eleven on each side actually took the field. The remainder sat down in long rows on benches and relapsed into a sort of alert coma.

Football in the United States is a cross between, and combines most of the less pleasing features of, Rugby Football and the World War. The goal-posts and the shape of the ball are as in the former, the general attitude of the participants towards their opponents as in the latter. The object, as in Rugby, is to score a touch-down in the enemy's territory and then to kick a goal. But the two main weapons of the Rugby players' arsenal are hardly used by the Americans. The swift series of lateral passes, from hand to hand, as the three-quarter backs come down the Rugby field in the long diagonal line, is quite unknown, and thus one of the greatest of all athletic spectacles is missing from the American game. On the asset side of the account, however, is the absence of Rugby's most infuriating tactic — the deliberate kicking of the ball out of the field of play. Is there any other game in the world in which such a thing is permitted? Has anyone ever seen Tilden, temporarily out of breath and anxious for a short rest, hit all the tennis balls over the grand-stand? Does Walter Hagen, finding himself in a tight corner, hit all his golf balls into an adjacent wood or ocean as it may be, and hold up the game until they can be retrieved and his opponent's temper is nicely frayed? However, all that is a diversion from the topic in hand.

The chief method of advance in American Football appeared to me to be as follows: One player hugs the ball to his bosom and flings himself into the thick of the enemy, what time his young playmates try to clear a path for him by selecting an antagonist and violently assaulting him. The antagonists either go down like ninepins, in which case the young gentleman with the ball is quite liable to advance several yards, or else they evade their would-be assaulters and, seizing the ball-carrier, hurl him to the ground, jump on him, kneel, lie, fall, or bounce on him, and the game is brought to a standstill. Umpires in white coats, white knickerbockers, white shoes and white caps with enormous peaks, and black stockings which alone mar a perfect *symphonie en blanc majeur*, come racing up, and the heap of bodies is disentangled. Corpses, if any, are removed, and the game goes on. Sometimes there is doubt about the exact spot on which the gentleman with the ball was massacred, and a great deal of scrutinizing and peering goes on. At first I thought the reason was a sentimental desire to inlay a small memorial tablet into the turf after the game was over, enumerating the virtues, if any, of the deceased, recording his parentage and place of birth, and any scholastic triumphs that may have, improbably, come his way, and concluding with one of those simple and moving epigrams from the Greek of Simonides which praise the heroism of those who died for their country. And for that reason, I thought, there was this desire to fix the fatal spot. I was quite wrong, of course. It appears that if the attacking side can advance ten yards in four bull-like rushes, they are entitled to four more bull-like rushes, to try to gain another ten yards. When, therefore, there is some uncertainty whether ten yards and one inch or only nine yards, two feet, and eleven inches have been gained, officials come racing out with surveying instruments, chains, stakes, theodolites, sextants, quadrants, and all the rest of the apparatus necessary for the literal exercise of geometry. In the meanwhile a staff of statisticians writes down the exact yardage that each young bull has gained in each battering-attack, so that on the following day a million fans may read with a thrill how Mr. Smith made football history by advancing from his forty-yard line no less a distance than eighteen inches, or how Mr. Jones, by an unparalleled display of swerving, dodging, and sidestepping, carved an inroad into the enemy's territory of a yard and a quarter.

But the supreme moment in football, for the irreverent spectator at least, is the Huddle. The team that has the ball and is about to try to bucket its way through, over, or under its adversaries for ten whole yards, goes into Conference, and this solemn affair is called the Huddle. They all go into a little circle, put their heads down, embrace each other round the shoulders, and generally give the impression that at any moment they may burst into Kiss-in-the-Ring, or dance with girlish charm round an imaginary mulberry-bush. It is a most engaging ceremony, and reminded me, for some reason, of many Council meetings of the League of Nations that I have attended. I am told that on these occasions of fraternal greetings, the quarter-back, or master-mind of the team, whispers his orders for the next variety of tactics. For example, he may say "Sixty-six B" and woe betide any of the team who, mixing up in his mind "Sixty-six B" with "A Hundred and Twenty-four and a half," ruins the whole play by scragging the opposing guard when he ought to have scragged the opposing tackle. There will be some pretty snappy words for him from the Coach afterwards.

Well, the game goes on. Now Princeton gain six yards and a half. Now Williams recover a foot of the lost ground. The wind whistles a shriller note than ever and the concrete has turned to a slab of ice and the watery sun has given up its pallid competition with the flying horsemen of the clouds. The whisky bottles pass from hand to hand and from lip to lip, faster and faster, backwards and forwards like a shuttle in a spinning-loom. From time to time a young man pitches forward from his slab and subsides, unconscious, among the feet of his neighbours. It is not for me to enquire whether his paralysis has been induced by an excess of external cold or internal warmth. He is carried out by his friends and deposited somewhere in safety. The cheer-leaders are still dancing frenziedly like crazy marionettes, and the substitutes, who have been delegated to relieve the incompetent, the halt, and the maimed, are warming up on the line, apparently trying to hit themselves under the chin with their knees. Princeton is leading handsomely, but the students and alumni of that great college are in despair. For Williams, with only a paltry little squad of about thirty warriors, have scored a touch-down, and it is the first time in many a long day that the Princeton line has been crossed. Shade of President Madison, once a student at Nassau! Shade of Woodrow Wilson, who went from the direction of the affairs of the college to the direction of the United States, and thence, for a brief hour, to the direction of the whole world except the United States Senate! Shade, if you like, of King William III (though his loyalties may have been divided between his Nassau and the lads from Williamstown)!

The minute-hand of the clock creeps to the hour. With three minutes left to play, the Princeton coach stops the game and despatches a fresh party of players into the arena. They have only three minutes in which to win immortal glory, but at least they will be able to gather their grandchildren round their knee as the twilight falls and the lamps are being lit and the cows are coming home to the byre, and tell them once more the old heroic tale of how they played for Princeton against Williams, way back in the 'thirties.

The game is over. The elegant young men have led their last cheer. The whisky bottles flash from hand to hand for the last time, and then we join the long shuffle to the car park.

I was able to identify the Coaches of the two teams, but among all the charmingly pretty girls who applied their carmined lips with such daintiness and such precision to the necks of whisky bottles throughout the game, it was impossible to detect the Coaches' lovely daughters. Nor did the quarter-backs assist me by running true to *Saturday Evening Post form*. Not once did they neglect the game to glance up at bright eyes in the stand. Not once did they blatantly sell the pass by arrangement with their future father-in-law. Instead of yielding to the sweet allure of Romance, they confined all their activities to huddling and homicide.

Twenty-six players were killed while playing football in the year of my visit. During the last four years a total of exactly one hundred and fifty have been killed. And this in spite of suits of padded armour and helmets and shin-guards and thigh-pieces. Personally I would prefer the cold slab in the Stadium to the one in the mortuary.

When we got back to New York City (having, by the way, been pinched with extraordinary neatness for speeding in the Holland Tunnel; there was no fuss simply a telephone-call from some invisible watcher and a cop waiting for us at the other end) we bought the evening papers and found that a college called St. Mary's had been narrowly defeated by the University of California at Los Angeles. As the St. Mary's team was referred to throughout the report as the Gaels, I naturally took a keen interest in their fortunes. After all, we Gaels, members of a dying race, must stick together all over the world. The Tartan (except the Campbell Tartan) Against All Else must be the slogan of the Clans until there is no more Tartan left. The names of the footballing Gaels were:

Strub	Elduayan	Schreiber
Meister	Yezerski	Michelini
Kordick	Pennino	Kellogg
Jorgensen	Fiese	

If anyone supposes that I have invented or exaggerated this list, let him write a respectful letter, enclosing a stamped and addressed envelope for the reply, to those ladies and gentlemen whose duty it is to keep the athletic records of St. Mary's College, and ask for a list of the players in the games against the University of California in the 'thirties.

The main defence of this extraordinary game is that it is a reflection in miniature of the essential fundamentals of the American character. The spirit which drove the Pioneers into the prairies, the deserts, and the mountains, is the same which launches the flying tackle at the racing adversary and which accepts injuries and endures suffering with a stoic fortitude. There is much to be said for this argument, and much to be said against it. The bull-like quality of the short, and usually futile, rushes against the wall of the defence may be described as a microcosm of Washington's tenacity at Valley Forge, of Lee's frontal attack on the Cemetery Ridge at Gettysburg, of Grant's dreadful battering at the impregnable defences at Spottsylvania and Cold Harbor, and of the heroism with which the new American armies flung themselves against the veteran machine-gunners in the Forest of the Argonne. All that may be true. And it might be added that there is also a dash of stupidity about it which slightly resembles the exploits of the brave but unfortunate General Custer. Certain it is that when a subtle and imaginative genius at last applied himself to the evolution of new and cunning devices in the game, the bull-headed rushers were completely baffled, and it took years before anyone else even faintly understood what the late Mr. Knute Rockne was up to, or how he achieved his sensational results. Is it significant that this great Football-brain was of Scandinavian origin, and that his work of revolutionizing football was achieved in a Catholic college? I do not know. I merely ask the Questions.

But the argument which, to my mind, demolishes the theory that football is symbolical of the American character is this: whatever may be said for or against it as a game, as a spectacle, or as training-ground for the youth of the country, no one can deny that it is, of all games in the world, *in excelsis*, the Team Game of Team Games. Every single movement, whether in attack or in defence, requires the active and instant co-operation of the entire eleven men. Each man has something to do all the time, whether it is just plain assassination or an intricate movement on the tips of his toes, and if one cog in the wheel fails to work, the machinery breaks down.

Now, go to any hundred-per-cent American and suggest to him that his great country was built up out of Puritanism and Prairies by the Team-Spirit. Bridling with ill-concealed indignation he will inform you that America was built up by the exact antithesis of the Team-Spirit. He will tell you that the watchword of the nation is, always has been, and always will be, Individualism. And that is not all. It is none of your ordinary Individualism, none of your decaying, sheep-like, European Individualism. No, sir. It is a Rugged Individualism. That is what it is. Rugged. And if you are prudent, you will hastily agree with him, for by this time there will probably be a wild glare in his eye, as though he had subconsciously reverted to the character of his great-grandfather, who was so individualistic that he walked by himself from Aroostook, Maine, to El Paso del Norte, and was so rugged that the tomahawks of the Piutes bounced off his skull and had to be sent away to have their handles straightened.

It would probably provoke a fatal catastrophe if you suggested that this rugged old gentleman would have played Kiss-in-the-Ring, or danced round the mulberry-bush, or whatever it is, with his colleagues, or would have unselfishly passed the ball to one of them in order to promote the fortunes of the Team, or would have allowed his movements to be dictated, his physical courage aspersed, the legitimacy of his birth called in question, and his private morals animadverted upon, by a hired Coach with however many beautiful daughters.

It is best not to embark upon such controversial matters, but simply to record the private opinion that American football, with its twin principles of Collaboration and War, has nothing whatever to do with the traditional American character, with its twin principles of Individualism and Peace.

As I write these words, another proof comes most opportunely to my hand, that this fierce game is alien to the peace-loving nature of the American citizen. It is the report, by one of the foremost sporting journalists in the country, of the Rose Bowl game. The journalist, obviously trying to lash himself into a suitably militaristic frame of mind for describing the play, compares one of the players to a "human howitzer" who throws the ball "from his rifle-shot hand" and then, after countering a "main spear thrust," proceeded to "uncover his main double battery" and "smashed through the defence like an antelope." Small wonder that Stanford "had no aerial net — no anti-aircraft fire to break up the Southern game."

If that is not the language of a pacifically minded gentleman, writing for a pacifically minded public which knows nothing, and cares less, about the jargon of Mars, then I will eat a Stetson.

CHAPTER THREE

"Stand up, tall masts of Mannahatta! stand up, beautiful hills of
Brooklyn!"

WALT WHITMAN

Shortly after returning home from the football-game, I had one or two more
opportunities of looking at New York, and each time I took a stroll, usually
on foot but once in a taxi.

After the first dazzle of the skyscrapers had slightly worn off and I had
grown a little accustomed to the beautiful and absurd things, there was more
leisure to stare at sights that were less impressive but none the less strange.
The Elevated Railroad, for example, is a weird contraption which lacks every
jot of the two qualities America yearns for. It has neither the swift, silent
efficiency of Modernity, nor the quiet dignity of Age. It is the sort of railroad
which I would have built if I had been mechanically minded and half-witted,
and it makes the sort of noise which would drown a fair-sized artillery
bombardment and which would make the national anthem of a tribe of
Congolese Africans, played *fortissimo* with old saws upon sheets of rusty tin,
sound like the love-song of a Tyrolean maiden on a spring morning. Here, as
in the Subway, you can buy the entire system for a nickel, which struck me as
a very moderate sum considering that it includes a fleeting glimpse, at a range
of approximately twelve feet, into about ten thousand domestic interiors as
you whiz past. It is a barbarous form of transport. The passenger might well
expect to find Voodoo being practised by the station officials, and a stall on
each platform where a sacred white cock may be purchased and a sacrificial
knife obtained from a slot-machine. There are those who consider the Street
Car more hideous than the Elevated as it clanks its dreary way along, but
it is a controversy which admits of a wide and unprofitable discussion. But
both sides are agreed that where you have a Street Car under an Elevated, the
savage scream and the dismal clank together, there you have an abnegation

of all the cultural dreams that Man has striven to realize throughout the ages. Third Avenue is a living proof that all Progress, except Progress backwards, and very occasionally sideways, is a vain chimæra.

Let us leave this painful subject. The New Yorker's best transport is his own legs. Next come the private automobile and the taxi, and after that the Fifth Avenue veterans. Bracketed last, a long way down the course, come the fearful triplets of dinginess and noise, the Subway, the Elevated, and the Street Car.

There is something either strange or comical to be seen on every block. At one moment it may be the offices of the Bartenders School, Incorporated, at another the shop of a gentleman who advertises a nice line in pants and Gabardines. A Rolls-Royce, sprinkled liberally with footmen and chauffeurs in livery, will find itself held up by the cart of an itinerant seller of gaily coloured mattresses, crying his wares in a Mediterranean accent and striking three Swiss sheep-bells all the time with the handle of a baseball bat.

Down by West Twenty-Third the cheerful calls of the urchins one to another, and the refined conversation of the dwellers in London Terrace (the largest apartment-house in the world, where the hall-porters are dressed in a sort of parody of the uniform of the London police), are punctuated by the melancholy clanging of the bells on the locomotives as the Pennsylvania trains go creeping out. They sound like a bell-buoy warning steamers against hidden death. Up on West Fifty-second the rows of dingy little houses, windows shuttered and grimy, doors splintered, iron railings all bent and rusty, are survivals of that epoch when the youth of a nation learnt to soak bad whisky and worse gin in speakeasies, and when an Anglo-Saxon race handed power and wealth on a platter to the scum of Naples and Sicily.

Down in West Third there is a colony of dingy shops each one of which is occupied by a manufacturer of hat-linings, and on the ornate bronze ceilings of the elevators of the Municipal Building you will find the Royal Arms of England. (Perhaps they are placed there ironically, for these elevators are the creakiest and jerkiest that I ever was in.)

On Park Avenue there is a shop called Barkis, Willing & Co., and the boxes for the mailing of parcels are not fastened down in any way, but just stand about loose and haphazard on the sidewalks, inviting an enterprising bandit to hoist the whole thing into a truck and drive off with it. The walls of the post offices are lined with the bulletins of the Department of Justice of wanted fugitives, with photographs, finger prints, criminal record, etc. so that, if you feel so inclined, you can write out your letter and study the faces of the most hideous thugs at the same time.

And if you are tired of walking, put your foot on a shoeblack's stool in Broadway and lean back against the wall, and watch the folks go hurrying up and down this strangest of all streets. You never know what you are going to see next. It is as fatal to generalize about Broadway as about the United States. Peanuts, shoeblacks, and cinemas are the commonest sights. A skyscraper stands side by side with a theatre built in the classic style with columns, capitals, and pediment, and advertised by a gigantic green jackboot, and next door may be a one-story wooden candy store, four feet by six. If New York is a miniature world, Broadway is a miniature New York. All the rushing haste is there, and yet you may see a saunterer; all the genius of the New World goes racing by, and yet you may see a Tibetan Lama in meditation; all the architects of the Twentieth Century may build a skyscraper, but you may see a log cabin beside it. Gaudy theatres and dismal poverty, sables and rags, glittering neon lights and dirty alleys, Broadway is like a New England hooked-rug, made up of any scrap that comes to hand.

But after all it is only a miniature. There are other things to see in New York than giant green jackboots on Hellenic architecture. A whole world separates the peanut-seller of Broadway from the maritime folk of South Street, that small beginning amid the coves of the island from which has evolved the greatest port in the world. It is only a hundred and fifty years ago that Catherine Slip and Coenties Slip were little creeks in the sand. But Broadway up by Seventieth and Eightieth streets neither knows nor cares who built the foundations of the port, any more than the Londoner of Kensington knows or cares two pins about the Port of London.

In order to avoid the reproach of writing about places that I had never seen, I made several attempts to get off Manhattan Island into some of the other boroughs. The statement that "you can't understand New York by looking only at Fifth Avenue" is only second in popularity at cocktail-parties to its elder brother, "You can't understand America by looking only at New York." I tried, or almost tried, them all. It was a dismal business. The Bronx came first and succeeded in impressing its personality no better than by leaving behind a memory of dingy little houses, badly paved streets, garish advertisements, factories, heaps of rubble, tumble-down warehouses, railroad cuttings, alley-ways, and a general atmosphere of seedy dilapidation. Queens, contrariwise, is full of open spaces, stretching in splendid procession with almost contiguous boundaries, for miles. Wide and clear under the sky, they put to shame the tenemental squalor of the Bronx, and serve as ventilators through which the citizens of Queens can breathe the air of Ocean. They march eastwards in healthy stateliness, these open spaces, Calvary Cemetery,

New Calvary Cemetery, Mount Zion Cemetery, Mount Olivet, the two Lutherans, Linden Hill Cemetery, Mount Carmel, Mount Neboh and again Mount Carmel, and Union Field Cemetery, to the Cemetery of the Evergreens, the Cypress Hills Cemetery, the Salem Field Cemetery, and the borders of Brooklyn. Further north there are two more of the open spaces of Queens, side by side in somewhat sinister proximity, the St. Michael's Cemetery and the Grand Central Air Port.

I never achieved Jersey City, except in rapid transit, as rapid as possible, to further fields. Many a time I gazed at it across the Hudson and resolved to cross over and explore the amenities of its innumerable railroad stations, but always my heart failed me at the sight of that grimy silhouette. Once I got as far as to board a ferry-boat, but it was no good. Just as the local Charon was about to cast off, I fled down the gangway with a hoarse scream, back to the sheltering bosom of old Mother Manhattan. It was a narrow escape, and I could appreciate at that moment the slightly melodramatic gesture of all those heroes of history who have knelt down and kissed the sand of one beach or another in their time.

But although Jersey City was thus shirked, perhaps as a sop to conscience because Jersey City was thus shirked, I took a great deal of trouble over Brooklyn.

Now Brooklyn has one distinction that raises it high above the dingy Bronx, above even the cemeterial Queens, and for all I know, and I should certainly think it probable, over Jersey City. It has all the noise, all the squalor, all the shabbiness of the others, and more than its share of the criminal sub-European element, but here and there the wanderer will come unexpectedly upon little blocks of eighteenth-century houses, unspoilt and as lovely as the day on which they were built. They are scattered about in side-streets and byways, and there are even one or two seventeenth century farmhouses still standing, I am told, presumably with a good deal of perplexity, in the heart of the borough. Columbia Heights, an eighteenth-century row that looks across the East River to the Manhattan skyline and over Governor's Island down the Hudson, must surely have the most stupendous views from its windows of any residential houses in the world. Life in Columbia Heights must be just a series of dashes from window to window. Now the *Berengaria* is coming slowly up to the Cunard dock; now a destroyer pulls out of the Navy yard and heads for the Atlantic; sometimes a ship will berth just below the house so that her foremast is almost in the dining-room, and sometimes the sunlight explodes in a blaze upon the top of the Empire State Building. Columbia Heights is no place for a writer or an artist unless he has a large private income from money invested in safe Government Bonds.

These beautiful old houses make the rest of Brooklyn seem very queer. For instance, Fulton Street, the main shopping street, is as queer a street as I ever saw in my life. As a general rule, a go-ahead, enterprising, commercial community will try to make its shopping centre as attractive as possible to those ladies and gentlemen who have money to spend and are showing a tentative disposition to spend some of it. The attraction may take the form of comfort, ease, and luxury, as in the premises of a Bond Street picture-dealer, or of ready accessibility, as in the Champs Élysées, or of tasteful and yet opulent window display as in the establishments of Messrs. Cartier, or of a wild picturesqueness as in the bazaars of Fez and Ferghana and Ispahan. Whatever the method, the theory is the same. The rich, already dallying, are to be allured into dallying one second too long so that in that last second they may yield to the enticement of the wares for sale.

Fulton Street, the chief bazaar of Brooklyn, is a long narrow street, flanked as in Paris or Ispahan or anywhere else, with the wares of the merchant. The department stores are as grand as anything on Manhattan and as brilliantly lit-up in the evening. But down the centre of the street runs the ubiquitous Street Car, painted just the same dingy fawn colour (though perhaps fawn is hardly the word to apply to this system of traction), and economizing just as rigidly upon lubricating oil, as anything on Manhattan, and above the Street Car roars and jangles the Elevated. Between the rails of the Street Cars and the sidewalks there is just room to squeeze an automobile, and to the lamp-posts and traffic-signal-posts are affixed severe notices, "No parking here" and "No cruising for taxis." These two notices, when considered separately from the other amenities of the street, might be taken as an ingenious device to entrap the rich. It is easy to drive to a store in Fulton, but, your car having been shoo-ed away and the cruising taxi being forbidden, it is almost impossible to get out again, and you might therefore spend more money than you intended, to the profit of the store-keeper and to the satisfaction of those political economists who would cure all our evils by a freer circulation of currency. This would be a plausible, almost convincing, theory if it were not for the Street Cars and the Elevated. No human being with the slightest endowment of artistic sensibility would remain in Fulton Street an instant longer than was absolutely necessary on his first visit. He would run away screaming (and nobody would hear him), on foot, rather than wait a moment for his Duesenberg, and would never revisit the accursed place. Ah! you say, but the rich have no endowment of artistic sensibility. But the rich, I reply shrewdly, have as good an endowment of ears as their neighbours. And anyway, I add, think of Andrew Carnegie. To which you very reasonably answer that you have no desire to think of Andrew Carnegie, and there the matter comes to an end. Nevertheless, I still maintain that, as a shopping street, Fulton is the worst I ever saw. And even now I have not come to the end of Fulton's monstrosities. To the East the street broadens out into a spacious circle, just as Fifth Avenue blossoms into Washington Square, and Piccadilly and the Élysées into the Circus and the Étoile. Here also the Brooklyners run true to form. For this circle is the meeting place, not only of innumerable Street Car tracks, but of no fewer than four elevated railways criss-crossing one another in a weird and hideous welter of shape and sound. Let us leave this grim subject.

Brooklyn is a city of small houses. There are streets and streets with nothing higher than two or three stories, and stately avenues are often lined with the most quaint little buildings. But the thing which at once stamps and explains Brooklyn is this: it is a city of more than two million inhabitants, and yet it only has four big hotels, and they are all jammed together in the once fashionable neighbourhood of the Heights. The fact is, of course, that nobody goes to Brooklyn for pleasure, and those who go for work are not the sort who live in big hotels. On the other hand, almost as many people seem to go there to die, as to Queens, for there are lots of splendid hospitals and quantities of cemeteries.

I walked slowly back in the evening, past the Walt Whitman house and across Brooklyn Bridge. The mist was a deep violet over the Chrysler Building, blessedly almost hiding it altogether, and the shadows of the swarming craft upon the East River were lengthening. A clatter of steam-hammers came faintly from the Brooklyn Navy Yard where a warship was lying, grey against the jumble of slums which seem to welcome the returning sailor all over the world, and a vast advertisement on the wall of a building announced "Largest Jewish Daily in the World", and just below me, on the next track of the bridge, rattled a Street Car labelled "King's Highway." What a city! For more than a hundred and fifty years its citizens have been piously celebrating its True Republican Principles, and its emancipation from the decadent, degrading, dismal, influence of Royalty. And yet it sees nothing funny or peculiar in a Street Car labelled "King's Highway." Again I say, What a city! What else can one say?

My last stroll in New York City, before setting out to conquer the interior of the country, was done by taxi. It began with a curious, probably unique, little scene. While being driven in a taxi home to my hotel at three o clock in the morning, I fell into conversation with the driver, an intelligent young Jew named, as his identification card inside the cab informed me, Isidore Grunbaum. (It is a great deal easier to talk to, and to be overheard by, a taxi-driver in New York than in London. The British cabman is cut off from his fare by glass, which makes the fare safe from eavesdropping and also makes him stand in the rain while giving his instructions and again when paying his dues.) On arriving at my hotel in Madison Avenue, I asked Mr. Grunbaum if he would drive me round the city for four hours on the following afternoon, for the sum of ten dollars. "Too much," replied Mr. Grunbaum; "I will do it for seven." "Nonsense," I said, "I'll give you ten." "I'll only take seven," he replied stubbornly. A compromise was, of course, reached. But surely it is the first case on record of a Scotsman offering too much to a Jew and the Jew refusing to take it.

Punctual to the minute, Isidore arrived that afternoon with his handsome black and scarlet cab and we started off. We went to some queer places and I saw some queer things. I saw the Bowery, famous to all Europeans as the legendary home of street-gangs and Boys, and now sunk into an irredeemable poverty. A shave costs three cents in the Bowery and a meal can be got for ten. Fifteen cents will buy a night's lodging in a common dormitory and another five secures you the privacy of a board a few feet high cutting off the rest of the dormitory. The shops are full of old junk, obviously the fragments of furniture of the evicted and the distrained, and every street looks like a street of sellers without any buyers. Thence into Chinatown, home of the laundry, and across into Centre Street where the Bridge of Sighs, high above a side-street, links, fatally, the Central Police Headquarters to the famous Tombs prison, a grim, pseudo-medieval fortress of dirty, dark-grey stones. Centre Street and the Tombs were in a fine frenzy at the time of my visit, for only the day before, a criminal had been brought from the Tombs across the Bridge of Sighs to be examined in the "line-up." He was the last of a row of prisoners, and he was handcuffed to the prisoner next to him. Disliking the whole procedure, and fain to be elsewhere, he had waited until attention was focused on some other scoundrel, and then had eased the hand cuff off his wrist and strolled out through the doors that are invariably kept locked and were found locked after his departure. He had not been seen since.

From the Tombs we rambled to the City Hall and thence to Orchard Street with its row of street-traders on each side, where in Isidore's words, "You can buy anything from a battleship to a button." The bargaining in Orchard Street seemed to be pretty intensive. Oriental eyes were flashing, and Levantine shoulders were being shrugged with a rapidity that would have put to shame a skilled player of the concertina. Voices were raised in expostulation and dark hands were gesticulating with a superb vehemence. "You ask the price of a pair of spectacles," explained Isidore, "and he says fifty cents. You offer him three cents, and after twenty minutes you compromise on a nickel."

In Greenwich Village we dived down a flight of steps into a small bar that was half full of the ordinary type of bar-frequenter, and half full of an "arty" crew, talking a little too loudly and looking aggressively unselfconscious. It reminded me of the "Cadogan Arms" and the "Six Bells", both in the King's Road, Chelsea, London, in the days when third-rate painters and first-rate models used to sit on high stools, and drink beer, and smoke cigarettes through enormous green cigarette holders, and protest with slightly raised voices that they were waiting, by appointment, for Augustus John.

Isidore and I leaned on the counter in a corner and he told me about himself and about New York. He was born in London, in the Whitechapel Road, but his father had emigrated three years later. Isidore had been trained to be a Rabbi, "and now I am a hack- man," he said. From training for the Rabbinate he drifted into cab-driving, and from cab-driving into business, and when his business failed in the great Slump, "I went back to my cab." Isidore owned his own cab and wrote a weekly article for a newspaper that was devoted to the affairs and interests of taxi-men.

Isidore's prose style, like Mr. Dizzy Dean's, runs to the vigorous and the picturesque. He carries a punch in both hands and is not afraid to use it. This is an extract from Isidore's column:

As A BROOKLYN HACKIE SEES NEW YORK

When will these cheap muzzlers and chiselers learn to hack like men, instead of blocking up traffic as they do around the various entrances of the Waldorf? ... Notice that the new traffic regulation prohibiting parking in the theatrical zone is again prohibited between 7.45 and 9 P.M... . Orchids to the cop who last Tuesday night at Broadway and 50th street gave justice to the hackie who was being shoved around on a closed line, by four would-be hackmen... . Willie, the dispatcher of the Alliance Cab, is now ill and his friends in the industry wish him a speedy recovery... . What is there to the rumour that the Alliance Garage will not be getting any new Paramounts? ... Hackstands around the Grand Central are nicely located. We would like more of them... .

And here is another:

TOWN TAXI DOINGS

Winey Ganzi, formerly president of the Town Taxi, found hacking so good that he has gone into the glove business. And Kid Skinzi got a forty-five cent call; fare had no money and gave him 25 (twenty-five count 'em) bottles of beer instead of the dough. They all had a party and Skinzi could of had a date if he wanted it.

It makes a professional author a little wistful to see a hackman, even if he is trained for the Rabbinate, muscle in on the literary racket with such pep and vim.

The New York hackman, said Isidore, has a pretty poor time in a good many ways, and the independent owner has to face the cut-throat competition of the big fleets, the Yellow and the Radio, as well. Hacking is lousy, said Isidore. A hackie can put in as much as twelve to sixteen hours a day and still make less than he would if he was on Relief. Isidore as an independent owner, and an acutely intelligent man, was keenly interested in the competition of the fleets, and after a good deal of beer in the Greenwich Village bar, we repaired to a Special Meeting of the Independent Owners, Isidore as a Delegate, myself posing as some thing pretty hot in London's hack-world. The meeting took place in a Downtown office and consisted of fifteen Jews, an Italian, an Anglo-Saxon and myself. The proceedings lasted three hours and consisted almost entirely of dialogue that ran on the following spirited sort of lines:

MR. ZUSCHELHEIM: Mr. Chairman, the only thing I ask of the company is that we should concentrate upon our common welfare and refrain completely from personalities, but I feel it my duty to say that Mr. Apfelbaum over there is nothing but a lousy crook. (*Uproar.*)

CHAIRMAN (Mr. Jacob): Order, order. I will not allow ——

MR. APFELBAUM (*striking a table and pushing his nose into Mr. Z.'s face*). And who was it swindled his firm out of the insurance premiums? (*Uproar.*)

CHAIRMAN: Gentlemen, We are here to co-operate ——

MR. Z: I will co-operate with anyone in the world, but not with Mr. Apfelbaum, who is the lousiest crook in New York. (*Uproar.*)

MR. WERNICK: No, sir, the lousiest crook in New York is Mr. Eisenpreis sitting right there besides you. (*Uproar.*)

MR. EISENPREIS (*shaking his fist at Mr. Wernick*): And what jail were you in when I was fighting the Independents battle last year? (*Uproar.*)

CHAIRMAN: Gentlemen, we are here to co-operate ——

MR. ZELTINGER: Mr. Chairman, I move that we resolve to co-operate to the utmost in defending ourselves to the utmost against unfair competition, but before I move it I want to know, Mr. Chairman, what rake-off you are getting out of this and who are you getting it from. *Pandemonium. Frantic waving of cheap cigars, this being, apparently, the Jewish Independent Taxi-Owners' favourite form of gesture. Only Isidore remains quiet. He whispers to me that he will bet me a dollar to a nickel that the only Resolution that will be passed will be a Resolution to do nothing.*

After three hours of slander and counter-slander, invective and counter-invective, accusation and counter-accusation, the meeting agreed upon a Resolution, moved from the Chair, and passed unanimously, "that a further meeting be called in a month's time, and that in the meantime nothing be done."

After that we went and drank some more beer and Isidore talked about rackets and gambles. He told me about the Clip-Joint Racket which depends for its existence mainly upon the inexhaustible supply of rich business men who arrive on the spree from Pittsburgh, and Cleveland, and St. Louis, and elsewhere, at the Pennsylvania and Grand Central stations and tell the taxi-driver to drive them to some place where they can enjoy themselves. If the driver is a respectable man, he will not risk his licence and will drop his fare at the Plaza or the Waldorf-Astoria. But if he is disreputable, he will drive his man to the Clip-Joint and return next day for his rake-off. Isidore told me about the big Slot-Racket, and the Number-Racket on the horse races, and the Italian-Racket of the Game of the Ten Cities, and the Harlem game which is so neatly organized that each street has its bet-collector who calls at every house every morning for the dimes.

"This city," said Isidore, "is built upon gambling. Each section has its own national game, beginning with Wall Street and working down through Poles, Italians, Czechos, till you get down to the nigger dimes."

"This city," said Isidore, "is plumb-full of rackets. I picked up a fare last April, that's eight months ago, and I drove him from East Ninth to Radio City. When he gets out he says I drove so badly that he's strained his back over a bump. There weren't any bumps, but wot-the-hell. You don't need real bumps to go to Court. You need a crook doctor and a crook lawyer. The next thing I knew was a claim for a thousand dollars. A month after that my insurance company went bankrupt. But wot-the-hell. The Courts are so full up of cases that it won't come up for another two years, and by that time I'll be bankrupt."

"Oh, I hope not, Mr. Grunbaum," I said politely. Isidore looked at me blankly. "How do you mean you hope not? If that case ever comes into Court I'll turn my cab over to my brother and go broke. I'm not going to pay a thousand dollars to that racket. Say, listen, do you know how dopers inject themselves if they haven't got enough money to buy a hypodermic? They take the biggest safety-pin they can find, and they jab it into their arm and leave it there until it makes a big enough hole to stay open... ."

I saw many things that day. I saw a Funeral Parlour, in the window of which the sole exhibit was an advertisement of a Grand Card Reception and Dance

41

at the Pennsylvania Hotel. I saw a large and handsome building which called itself Educational Building. There was a show-case at the entrance to it, and in the show-case there were three books called, *Murder in Bermuda*, *Death in the Theatre*, and *Death of an Honest Broker*. We hastened on. I had no desire to investigate the curriculum, nor interview any of the professors who lectured on such startling subjects. I saw a sudden wave of beauty, carrying more pretty girls on each yard of its crest than six blocks of Fifth or Park Avenue ever carry in the daytime, which showed us that the staff of Macy's Department Store had just been dismissed from its work, and in Union Square we paused for a moment to listen to an orator addressing a crowd under the shadow of Lafayette's elegant statue (though it is surely a poor compliment to the swordsmanship of that great man to make him grasp the blade of his sword so firmly) and at the end we rounded the Washington Arch, with its rows of lovely old red brick houses on each side, and there in front of us was the long stretch of Fifth Avenue rising slowly towards the sky and then falling away over the hill into the dove-blue shadows of the evening.

While I was wandering through Manhattan's semi-practical, semi-romantic street-system, now gazing with admiration at the front of the Players Club, now shocked by the Lady Chapel of St. Patrick's Cathedral, at one moment enchanted by the old houses in Grove Street or Macdougal Alley, at the next running with loud screams away from the brown horror of the Fifth Avenue Presbyterian Church, I missed one whole class of place-names. I could not find a Bunker Hill Avenue, nor a Yorktown Park, nor a Saratoga Railroad Station, nor a Concord Bridge, nor any other record of the defeats of the British Arms. There is no flaunting in New York of the miserable scuttlings and surrenderings of the Royal Armies, as London flaunts its Waterloo and Trafalgar, and Paris the hundred great victories of France. And it would appear that the spirit which prefers the everyday work of peace to the advertisement of ancient slaughters is still dominant, because I could not find an Argonne Avenue or a St. Mihiel Boulevard, or anything more bellicose than a few memorials to famous soldiers, a bridge and a square for Washington, a square for Pershing, a tomb for Grant, and for Sherman an equestrian statue, advancing cautiously to battle in the Plaza behind the petticoats of a well-developed lady.

CHAPTER FOUR

Where the Katy-did works her chromatic reed on the walnut-tree
over the well.

WALT WHITMAN

The pious tourist has always his Mecca. For the American in England it is
Stratford-on-Avon. For the Englishman in the East it is the Club. For the
Frenchman anywhere it is France, and for all children of the British Empire
in London it is Lord's cricket-ground. As a pious British tourist in America,
therefore, I paid the customary visit of ceremony to Harlem. This invariable
homage to Central Africa is the outcome of three strong forces. Firstly, there
is the power of Tradition, to which no country accords a greater deference
than Great Britain. Every British traveller has always been to Harlem, and so
every British traveller will always continue to go to Harlem. It is one of the
things that are "done." In the next place, when he returns to Great Britain, the
first, and often the only, question that will be put to the traveller is, "Did you
go to Harlem?" If he falters, stammers a little, and replies, "Well, not exactly,"
there will be a painful silence and then a change of conversation. I was once
present in the smoking-room of a Club in St. James's Street when a friend of
mine named Smith entered with a guest named Brown and addressed himself
to a somnolent lieutenant-general named Robinson as follows: "General, let
me introduce Mr. Brown. Mr. Brown has been living in New York for the last
thirty years."

"Ah! Mr. Brown", replied the courteous old boy. "Thirty years in New
York, eh? Did you go to Harlem?"

And the third reason which attracts the citizens of the Empire to Harlem
is a lively, and quite understandable, curiosity to view some coloured folks
who do not dwell under the beneficent shadow of that Empire's flag. It is
always a faint surprise to the British when any of these are actually visible
to the naked eye, and it is well worth a pilgrimage to have a look at them. I
duly went to Harlem and so qualified for the green turban. Green is the right

word. For I went in the small hours of the morning to a night-club that was run entirely to attract strangers and mugs like myself, and I saw of course just as much of the real Harlem as a traveller sees of the African jungle by sitting in the cocktail-bar of a Union Castle liner in the harbour of Cape Town. And this was a pity, for Harlem is unique, a centuries-old African kraal in the middle of the great Progressive capital of the West. The houses look as if they are made of stone, but all the same they are, if you look at them properly, primaeval huts. Harlem may be only three hundred years old historically, but the spirit is the spirit of the ageless jungle. But the ordinary, casual visitor can get to know nothing of it. If he wanders through the district in the daylight, he sees nothing but a district populated by blacks instead of whites, hastening on the small round of daily tasks in just the same way as anyone else, while if he wanders the streets at night he has the choice of rambling where he likes and probably getting his throat cut with a razor, or else of keeping to the well-defined, beaten track and going to the artificial night-clubs which cater for him just as the cafés in Montparnasse and Montmartre used to cater for the Anglo-Saxon tourists in the days when the pound and the dollar were worth a pound and a dollar.

The dressed-up cafés and cabarets of Harlem are loathsome places, in which the fastidious visitor does not dislike and despise the negro singers and dancers quite so heartily as the negroes themselves dislike and despise the white singers and dancers. Thick African lips twist contemptuously at the pretty youths who caper about in feminine dress, and the barbaric rattle of drums which once called the warriors to war now accompanies a painted and fetching young man in his obscene contortions. The honest Dutch burghers who built the village of Harlem would be surprised if they could see it now.

Party followed party. High-ball followed high-ball. Day by day the pace grew faster and faster. Week by week my collection of honorary memberships of Clubs grew larger and larger. But the autumnal leaves were turning to "crimson and russet and olive and gold," and the first faint hints of frost were in the early morning air, and the breezes from the Atlantic were no longer laden with the balm and myrrh of the Gulf Stream, and Hannibal, if I may compare myself to that illustrious soldier, was still dallying in Capua. Above the din of the Elevated a new and steady hum was gathering in volume every day, the tinkle of many silvery voices repeating, "You can't understand America by looking only at New York." People began to ask, innocently, "When are you leaving?" And as a topic for conversation my Proposed Itinerary began to oust Reminiscences of Prohibition and even, so strong was Public Feeling in the matter, "Depression; Will it last for Ever?" And when I heard that at some tables it was running neck and neck with the Iniquities of the President, it became painfully clear to me that I must make a move. The only problem was, In which direction should that move be made?

It was not that there was any dearth of Advice on the matter. On the contrary. The world seemed as anxious to get me out of New York as it had seemed to be delighted to get me in, and amateur Itinerarians were plentiful. For it is a subject — the Itinerary of travelling writers — upon which, as upon so few others, Americans not only feel very strongly, but hold clear-cut views that are not befogged by the amiable sentimentalism of the national character. They are indignant enough rather unjustly, as I have already shown — when British authors slink home from a whirl of New York gaiety and then throw quarts of vitriol at America. But what really annoys them is their belief that British authors do not even take the trouble to go and look at the places which will ultimately become the targets for the corrosive liquid.

"A week in New York," said innumerable charming ladies to me with a most engaging vehemence, "a week in Boston, a day in Philadelphia, a football-match, and a week-end on Long Island, and you Britishers think you know America."

"No one can know America," said innumerable charming ladies to me, "unless they have seen Atlanta, Georgia," or it may have been Charleston, South Carolina, or Seattle, or the Golden Gate at San Francisco, or Wisconsin, or Martha's Vineyard, or any one of five hundred places each of which seemed to be at least a thousand miles from any of the others. But after a bit I began to get the different attractions classified into sections. Thus in Section One there were five that "of course you will be going to see, Mr. Macdonell." These were New Orleans, Washington, The Century of Progress Exposition at Chicago, the Grand Canyon of the Colorado River, and the top of the Empire State Building. Whenever Section One was broached, I set my teeth and smiled a sort of smile and swallowed the burning words that I longed to speak, and nodded and said, "Oh, of course I shall be going there," and at last I swore a great and binding oath that I would not visit New Orleans, or Washington, or the Century of Progress Exposition at Chicago, or the Grand Canyon of the Colorado River, or the top of the Empire State Building. Nor did I. The oath was truly kept.

In Section Two came the large towns of the Union, and the advocates of this section tried to make me believe that I would learn about America by visiting Philadelphia, Pittsburgh, Cleveland, Buffalo, Detroit, St. Louis, Kansas City, Rochester, Milwaukee, Cincinnati, and a score of others. But when I enquired in respect of what quality any of these towns was different from any other no one could answer. And when I enquired in respect of what quality any of these beastly new American industrial towns differed from any of our beastly new European industrial towns, again no one could answer. So I, who have seen England's Sheffield, Scotland's Glasgow, France's Lille, Germany's Essen, Italy's Turin, and many another abominable mass of chimneys and slums and hurrying, mean-faced humanity, drew a pencil through the whole of Section Two.

Section Three was much more difficult to deal with, as it was composed of the home-towns either of the people I met at parties, or of the grandfathers or aunts or cousins of the people I met at parties. Thus I was incessantly being called upon to assess in my mind the comparative merits of such places as Burlington, Iowa, Evansville, Indiana, Peoria, Illinois, and Guthrie, Oklahoma. I was given to understand that I had only to set foot in any of them and the town would stop work for the duration of my visit. But it was too difficult to choose from so many, and in the end I had reluctantly to eliminate Section Three.

The Itinerary in Section Four was entirely guided by the letters of introduction with which I was showered in New York. From a study of the august names upon the envelopes of these letters, it appeared that there was no necessity for me to associate on my travels with anyone beneath the rank of a State Governor or the President of a University. Section Four, therefore, was torn up at once, and when I set out at last from New York it was on an Itinerary of my own, combined and dovetailed with three other Itineraries drawn up by the three gentlemen to whom this book is dedicated.

If the Viscount Howe had taken as much trouble over his staff work when he set out from New York in 1777, he might have obtained more successful results against General Washington.

But before I actually set out on the Grand Tour, I made one small excursion out of New York, to get acclimatized, so to speak, to the atmosphere of the countryside. My objective was the country near Westport, Connecticut, and I managed to choose a pouring wet day for the excursion. Friends came for me with an automobile, and we drove out through Harlem and the Bronx, which seemed even drearier than ever in the rain, and past a jumble of shacks and sheds and filling-stations, and out on to a great broad road through dripping woods. The scenery changed quickly from grand urban to squalid urban, then to suburb and squalid suburb, then to woodland which is waiting to be ruined, at a vast number of dollars per acre, by someone rich enough and beastly enough to want to convert lovely woods into loathsome buildings, and then to richer suburbia, houses standing separately in small patches of woods, and a bewildering network of broad concrete roads. After that came the first beautiful architecture, the real old New England houses, with their wooden boarding (exactly as you will find in the farmhouses in Kent, old England) and their porches of dainty Greek columns with severe Doric capitals, and their spotless whitewash and always green shutters of that lovely dusty green that you find in Provence and in Cézanne's pictures. They are dignified and unflamboyant and simple, and they make their modern garish neighbours look even more hideous that the poor things deserve.

We plugged on through the rain, now passing smart yacht-clubs on the Sound, now running between sad-looking stooks of greyish corn in the fields, and stopping from time to time for lunch at famous restaurants, cafés, and roadhouses, and finding that all were shuttered, bolted, and barred. The Season was over and that feeling of damp melancholy had descended which always makes a fashionable resort, when the Season is over, a far drearier thing even than a Scottish moor at twilight, when a mist is creeping up from the sea and the curlews are crying to each other and there is no human habitation north, south, west, or east, for miles and miles and miles. And Gaiety has the habit of leaving behind it not only the sadness of departed fun but also a great many broken bottles and old tins.

At last we found a restaurant that was open, a celebrated house for fish called Clam Allen's, and there I ate for the first time clam chowder, and then what seemed to be several hundreds of steamed clams, and then half a broiled lobster, and then I felt better. Clam Allen's is a small wooden house so near the edge of the bay on the Sound that the guest who lunches in the window looks straight down into the water a yard below him. Clam Allen's is the fishiest and the most maritime restaurant I have ever been in. The walls were decorated with models of sailing-ships and the steering-wheel of a motor-boat. Over our heads there was a gallery in which the fishing-nets were stored, and just outside were the floating tanks for the clams and lobsters. Beyond the tanks, gulls wailed mournfully over the reeds, and the rain fell steadily out of a grey sky. In the distance across the bay an old stone barn was faintly visible, looking like the small fortress of some early settler. But by the time we had reached the broiled lobster we did not care in the slightest how hard it rained, or what dirge the seagulls chanted, and for the rest of my life I shall never understand why a derogatory sense should be attached to the adjective "clammy."

The woods above Westport were full of the tinkling sound of little streams, and the tawny splendour of the maple leaves was reflected in hundreds of little pools, and the birch-trees glistened in the rain, and a hot vapour rose steadily from the sodden moss and the last year's leaves. Great clumps of what we call in England Michaelmas Daisies were growing wild on the banks, and here and there dark outcroppings of rock steamed in the sultry heat. A grasshopper with black wings to help his already efficient legs came leaping past, and as the sun sank the crickets began to tune up their evening orchestra.

From a hill covered with pines we could see below us a dark mysterious lake, surrounded with trees to its very edge and drained by a tiny sluice that murmured away like the sound of bees. Everything was dark, the trees and their shadows and their reflection on the still water, except only a vermilion canoe which lay in a small clearing on the bank and cast a vermilion picture of itself on to the lake.

Eastward in the distance lay a band of evergreen trees shutting out the world except at one gap through which shone the waters of the Sound, with Long Island dim on the horizon. The Sound was touched for a moment by a glint from the setting sun, and a three-masted schooner lay becalmed upon it.

Early next morning I bathed in the dark mysterious lake and was told afterwards by genial friends that they were so sorry that they had forgotten to warn me that it was full of snapping turtles.

CHAPTER FIVE

City of ships!
(O the black ships! O the fierce ships!
O the beautiful sharp-bow d steam-ships and sail-ships)

WALT WHITMAN

It is one of the peculiarities of the Grand Central Station in New York City that whereas it is possible to buy hats, oysters, diamonds, umbrellas, shoes, flowers, silk-stockings, caviare, and toys under its hospitable roof, and probably, for all I know, wooden legs as well, and suspension bridges, artificial teeth, battle cruisers, and parrots, nevertheless it is almost impossible to find any trains. The main central hall is rather like a cathedral. The high roof, the great glass window, the hushed sound of voices, the shuffle of feet, and the black porters in their red caps, all give the impression that here is some oriental mosque, or church in Abyssinia perhaps, and that at any moment a Patriarch in gorgeous vestments may appear at the top of the steps and recite a Coptic benediction. But wait you never so long you will see nothing more exciting than a notice predicting that a local train to Bronxville will be starting at 10.40 A.M., though whence it will be starting is another matter. The platforms and the trains are kept carefully hidden from enquiring eyes.

It was therefore with no sense of disquiet that I began my search in the station of the Baltimore and Ohio Railroad in Forty-second Street for a train that would take me to Baltimore. The fact that no trains were visible was not a matter for alarm. It was just a question of perseverance before I succeeded in running them to earth, and a guarantee of my ultimate success was I felt it reasonable to assume, contained in the illuminated sign outside the station which said "Baltimore & Ohio Railroad" and also in the series of advertisements in a window in the street which assured the prospective traveller to Baltimore that something pretty sensational in the railroad comfort line was awaiting the lucky fellow.

But when at the end of twenty minutes, these super-trains were still eluding me, and the whole station was wrapped in the deepest and most slumberous silence, I began to get a little anxious, and I accosted an official. The following dialogue took place:

MYSELF (*politely*): Can you tell me, please, where I can find the 10.30 train to Baltimore?

OFFICIAL (*with old-world courtesy*): The ten-thirty bus, sir, leaves from the end of that passage which leads into Forty-first Street.

MYSELF: I fear you mistake my meaning. I refer, not to a bus, but to the 10.30 train.

OFFICIAL: That's right. 10.30 bus. At the end of that passage.

MYSELF (*as one reasoning with a charming but rather stupid child*): No, no, my good man. The train. Train to Baltimore. Baltimore, a city on Chesapeake Bay. Metropolis of Maryland.

OFFICIAL: That's it. Bus.

MYSELF: Train.

OFFICIAL: Bus.

MYSELF: Hell!

I gave it up, consoling myself with the reflection that a nation which calls a Tram a Trolley-car, Petrol Gasoline, and a Lift an Elevator, is perfectly capable of calling a Train a Bus. I therefore went patiently into a waiting-room near the end of the now almost famous passage into Forty-first Street and sat down. After a few minutes, quite incredibly, a sliding door opened and there stood a handsome green bus, labelled Baltimore. I clambered in, settled myself down for a very long drive, and was soon immersed in a bundle of those enormous magazines which contain two complete novels, ten short stories, twenty articles, and a hundred pages of advertisements, all so inextricably jumbled up and interwoven one with another that it is quite impossible to find one's way about. I was just struggling to disentangle a story of Strong Men on the Frontier from a grim picture of a Young Woman who was asking herself "Why did he not kiss me a second time in the Rose-Garden?" when I became conscious that the rattling motion of the bus had given place to a soothing, quiet roll from side to side and, looking up from that poor tortured face, I found to my astonishment that we were now on a ship in the Hudson River, and apparently laying a course for Europe. By this time it was lamentably clear that whatever difference of language may conceal the identity of the Tram and the Trolley, no one could suppose that I, on the one hand, and, on the other, the Baltimore & Ohio Railroad Company saw eye to eye on what did, and what did not, constitute a train. It was possible, of course, that I was being tactfully deported as an undesirable alien, but a sort of Scottish vanity buoyed me up with the alternative notion that I was going to make the journey to Baltimore entirely by sea. But in that case there was little point, from the economic angle, in carting the whole bus down by sea too. Surely there must be buses in Maryland that could meet us at the other end of our voyage; or perhaps there was a strike of the Maryland bus-drivers; or perhaps — but all these meditations were cut short by the old familiar view — the Downtown skyscrapers. Seen from mid-river opposite about Thirtieth Street they look like the outline of a medieval fortress, guarding the entrance to a country as Elsinore guards the Danish Sound and Bouillon watches the Marches of the Ardennes. In the sunlight each skyscraper has a little plume of white steam blowing from the summit, like Everest and its plume of driven snow.

Our ferry-boat turned a little and made for the New Jersey coast and soon we were tying up to a Quay. The bus sprang into life again and, the moment that the gang plank was down, ran ashore and pulled up beside what everyone, including myself and the B. & O. Railroad Company, would agree was a real honest-to-God train.

A few minutes later a black man had seized my hat and put it into a large brown-paper bag, and we were sliding smoothly through the squalid and tumble-down suburbs of Jersey City.

Coming from New York to Baltimore, the eye at once misses, and the neck also, the skyscrapers. There is only one tall building in the whole city, and it was somehow with an especial glow of pleasure that one learnt the story of that tall building. It had been a bank, and Mammon had raised its towers up to Heaven just as those other folk who "had brick for stone, and slime had they for mortar, and who said, Go to, let us build us a city and a tower, whose top may reach unto heaven." And when the great Slump came, the bank with the tall tower was the first of all the institutions of Baltimore to close its doors and go bankrupt. On hearing this story I would normally have laughed a great deal, but I had not been long enough in Baltimore to compile the list of subjects at which the foreigner may not laugh in the presence of Baltimoreans. Later on, I found that in this cheerful city you may laugh at anything you like, and that the Baltimorean, as a rule, will not join in your laughter because he will have started to laugh before you.

Apart from this one tall northern building, the city is of a southern or European altitude, and I soon found that this union of North and South is the thread that runs through every corner of the Baltimorean pattern. It meets the eye first, naturally, in the architecture. The high vaunting ambition of the skyscraper is the contribution of Manhattan with its passionate desire to be bigger or more startling or more efficient than any thing else in the world. The architectural contribution of the South is the supremely beautiful

51

Colonial style of building which reaches its perfection in Homewood, the house of Charles Carroll of Carrollton, just outside the city. The skyscraper and Homewood, these are the symbols of the two types of civilization which meet and mingle in Baltimore, and they spread through the whole life of the community. Between them they have made Baltimore a city of bustling commercial activity and Beethoven string-quartets, of oil refineries and one of the greatest medical schools in the world, of modern American democracy and of old- world Cavalier culture, of vast warehouses and of packs of fox-hounds. Businessmen go hustling along, but they have time to stop for a laugh. The tankers go chugging down Chesapeake Bay, but if you wait an hour or two you will see a four-masted ship with dark red sails go slipping out to the Ocean. Everywhere there is the mingling of North and South. There is pride in the past as well as pride in the present, and the Baltimorean has hit upon the secret, hidden, I think, to every other State in the Union, of being an aristocratic democrat.

Intensely American he is proud of George Calvert. Fourth among the States to publish its Declaration of Rights, Maryland prizes much of the English aristocratic tradition. For it does not forget that it was no lantern-jawed Puritan, nor meek Quaker, nor slave- trader, nor concession hunter, nor illiterate pioneer, who founded the State of Maryland, but a catholic Gentleman who had once been Secretary of State in England, and who, when he had to choose a name for his foundation, called it after that daughter of Henry, King of Navarre and France, who became the Queen of England.

There may be a Washington County at one end of the State but there is a Queen Anne County at the other. There is Franklinville, but do not overlook the town called Princess Anne, and if on one side of the Patuxent River there is the sturdy, democratic homeliness of Mechanicsville, it is balanced on the other side by the courtly elegance of Prince Fredericktown.

To return to the Carroll house. The stranger, trying to gain a glimpse into the heart of this gay and sunny city — not for nothing is Baltimore's world-famous newspaper called *The Sun* — would do well to concentrate for a while upon Homewood, for it has a treble importance.

Firstly, it is a sign to all the people of Baltimore that they need not be worried by the Northerner's obsession about Antiquity. Nor are they. At their doors stands this perfect example of the architecture of Colonial times. Secondly, Homewood has its own individual beauty, with its old, rose-pink bricks, its two delicately proportioned wings and its square, white porch pedimented and pillared with four Grecian columns that taper slenderly to simple capitals. Built a hundred years after Queen Anne, yet it is full of the spirit and line of the best of Queen Anne, with the colouring of the earlier Carolean, and the classical touch in the Hellenic porch. The third importance of the Carroll house is that it has served as a model for succeeding generations of Maryland architects. Elsewhere architects have succumbed to temptation and have built great turreted and pinnacled châteaux of the French Loire on Long Island, pseudo-Gothic monstrosities in the streets of London, and European palaces at New Delhi. But the men of Baltimore are made of sterner stuff. They have stuck doggedly to the use of a Maryland model for Maryland buildings, and not, as you might have expected, the German style of Herr Peter Behrens, or the Swedish style of Mr. Östberg, or the London style of Sir Christopher Wren, or any other imported style.

So you will continually find beautiful examples of modern Colonial architecture in and around Baltimore, based on the Carroll house. The whole of the Johns Hopkins University, for instance (which incidentally owns Homewood), is built on variations of the famous model, and there is a residential district in which the plans of every new house have to be passed by a committee of architects who are obviously strong adherents of the old Colonial. The result is that each house in this quarter is not only a beautiful modern building in itself, but is also harmonious with all the rest. Guilford is a fine example of town-planning as it ought to be. (Later we shall come to a fine example, in another city, of town-planning as it ought not to be.)

In between the period of the Carroll house and the modern disciples of Carrolldom come the rows of small, neat, domestic, Baltimorean houses, made of brick and seldom more than three storeys high. They have a queer complacency of their own, which may be due to their middle-class smugness, or to the dark red paint with which the brick-work is heavily coated a *décor* which is surely unique on such a large scale. For myself I prefer to think that the sleekness of these little dwellings is another example of Nature following the guidance of Art, and that they were not really quite so complacent, quite so individually sleek, until they heard that Henry James had written of them as "little bird-faced and protrusively door-stepped houses, which, overhung by tall, regular umbrage, suggested rows of quiet old ladies, with their toes tucked-up in uniform footstools, under the shaded candlesticks of old-fashioned tea-parties." After that exquisitely felicitous picture, no one in his senses will ever try to re-describe for posterity Baltimore's painted brick houses and polished door-steps.

The key-point to Baltimore's history is Fort McHenry, a lovely old red brick fort on the point which dominates the entrance to the inner harbour. The architect who built Fort McHenry had an eye as keen for aesthetics as for strategics. The design of the central part with its white pillars and its dainty hexagonal powder magazines is almost on a level with the Carroll house itself. It was here that the British attempted to surprise the town in the idiotic war of 1812-1814 (in which neither side knew when the war began, when it was finished, or what it was all about anyway) and were repulsed so vigorously that they forthwith abandoned the attempt to capture Baltimore.

This was the occasion on which Mr. Francis Scott Key was so elated at the defeat of the Union Jack that he sat down there and then and composed "The Star-Spangled Banner." Whether or not the British contributed to the poetical advancement of the world, by providing the inspiration for this composition, is a matter of opinion. Certainly it might have been better for both countries if Baltimore had been captured on that occasion and humanity thus spared such lines as "Their blood has washed out their foul footsteps pollution." But it was not to be. In the picturesque words of the British General Ross it "rained militia," the Peninsular veterans were driven back, and Mr. Key's poetical fancies were loosed upon the world. Baltimore itself has provided a comment which I, as a stranger, would never have dared to make. For a tall flagstaff marks the fatal spot where the Muse descended upon Mr. Key, and the Baltimoreans have erected a large bronze statue, either of Apollo or of Orpheus — I am not sure which — with his back ostentatiously turned to the flagstaff.

The view from Fort McHenry is superb. All the long reach of Chesapeake Bay stretches out before you with its wooded shores that fade their thin, dark outlines into the haze of the Atlantic. In the far distance you can see the outline of the island which the greatest of American soldiers and gentlemen, then plain Colonel R. E. Lee of the United States Engineers, made into a fort. Beyond that are the fairy-like cranes and towers and spidery derricks of steel-works. The water of the bay is dotted with craft. Ferry-boats and tugs potter about busily. Oil tankers strike the note of Modernity, while Antiquity is served by barquentines plying gracefully along, as the clippers used to ply that brought glory and wealth to Baltimore and carried grain to Europe. And if you are lucky you may see a tiny racing craft go reeling past with all canvas set, and a nigger perched on each of the eight out riggers to try to keep the balance. And if you are luckier still you may see the racing-craft haul up a shade too closely into the wind, and over she swings and presto! eight niggers are in the water and nobody cares a tinker's damn what becomes of them. There are plenty more where they came from. Indeed there are plenty of Africans in Baltimore, that City of North and South, and they are Northern enough in spirit to possess a certain civic sense and there is enough of the North in Baltimore to give the negro certain opportunities for culture and prosperity, and at the same time they are Southern enough in spirit to be dominated by the tradition, the not so very old tradition, of slavery, and there is enough of the South in Baltimore to keep the memory of that domination alive.

The negro in Baltimore steadily prospers, and like all sub-races, he steadily eats his way into the residential quarter of the City. Just as the Jew pushes the Gentile, so the negro pushes the Jew. Harlem Square, that beautiful open square with the fine old houses all round, is entirely black now, and there are strong stone synagogues left isolated, like rocks in an advancing tide of darkness, in streets where neither American nor European nor Asiatic now dwells.

But not all the Africans live in large handsome houses. The negro slums, only a yard or two from the active, cheerful centre of the City, have to be seen to be believed. Leeds and Wolverhampton and Sheffield, industrial towns of England, have nothing to compare with these foul alley-ways, often less than a yard wide, with their wooden shacks jammed back to back against each other, and the tiny lanes of wretchedly made bricks that crumble before your eyes. If you waited for an hour in front of one of these brick hovels, if you could stand the smell and the atmosphere of venerable garbage, and the dreary, scavenging cats, I swear you would see a brick fall out of a wall, or a door-lintel crumble into dust or a window frame sag under its own weight. Sometimes one of the cracked and peeling doors is open and, as you pass, a great cloud of vapour, partly the smell of cooking and partly the odour of long decay, human and material, strikes you in the face. On the floor of the room, if you have the moral courage and the physical insensibility to pause and look, half a dozen negroes are playing cards with a pack that was once white and now is as dingy and crumpled as themselves. Or they may be throwing dice with strange and wonderful exhortations to the dice and imprecations to Fortune. But whatever they are doing, you may be sure that the floor space is fully covered by the half reclining, elbow-resting forms. In a room six feet by six, half a dozen negroes will somehow find the space to twist the pasteboard or roll the ivory.

And round the corner is the hurrying, gay, sunny City, the Commercial, the Cavalier.

I am not concerned in this book in writing about historical events nor in writing about great public buildings, whether in Baltimore or anywhere else, and in any case Karl Baedeker would describe them with a far greater accuracy and in a more concise language. So I will say nothing of the great square Hall of the War Memorial, surely ranking with the War Memorials in Edinburgh and Winchester College and Charterhouse School for stateliness and grandeur, nor of the frescoes round its walls by the painters of Maryland, nor of the dark shot-tower behind it, nor of the Enoch Pratt Library, nor the Washington Column, nor even the Johns Hopkins University.

I am much less interested in the handsome new Pennsylvania Railroad Station and the huge project of electrifying the whole track from New York to Washington, than in the shadowy little Calvert Station, the oldest station in the United States, obscure and dilapidated, to which Abraham Lincoln came from his home in Illinois on his way to Washington to be inaugurated as President of the United States. He was not liked in Maryland in those days, and the legend runs that he arrived disguised as a woman to avoid being pelted by the mob while he changed from the Illinois train to the Washington train.

There are many fine shops in Baltimore, but I prefer the tiny place in which you can buy a glass-eye, choosing your own colour, for ten dollars, or the window which proudly announces that in the premises behind it you will find the World's Master Craftsman in Memory Stones. A few yards from the Craftsman is the office of the Grand Sachem of the Maryland Improved Order of Red Men, whatever in the name of wonder that means, and everywhere there are small tailors and small pawnbrokers. These are without question the two main industries of Baltimore.

Every little street is full of them, and there is a magnificent opening here for a series of vaudeville jokes on the ancient theme of pawning the Sunday trousers. Perhaps each tailor is also a pawnbroker or *vice versa*, and re-sells as new, in the one establishment, the trousers which a client has failed to redeem in the other. This, if true, would be a remarkable, indeed probably unique, example of the Vertical Trust.

Then there are the Churches. The place is full of them, of every denomination from Catholic down to, or up to, depending on which you belong to, the African Methodist Episcopal. One of the splendid legacies of George Calvert, first Baron Baltimore, was the tradition of Religious Toleration within the Christian Religion, and it is a legacy which Maryland has treasured for three hundred years. I say advisedly "within the Christian Religion," because if you talk of this Maryland tradition of Toleration to a Jew, the mildest reply he is likely to make is, "What toleration?" But, without taking one side or the other in that sort of controversy, I make no question that Maryland was far ahead of England, and is still centuries ahead of some parts of Europe, in its broad-minded spirit towards the different sects which claim to be the one true Christian Religion. From time immemorial each Christian man and woman has worshipped in Maryland as each Christian man and woman has wanted to. In consequence there are hundreds of Churches in Baltimore, and the Spirit of Toleration has even spread to the ecclesiastical architecture, which is almost sensationally variegated. The City must have been submerged by wave after wave of architectural fashion, and, to make it worse, the waves do not seem to have arrived in strict chronological order. In Europe it is quite common to see a church in which Norman has succeeded Saxon, and Perpendicular has been grafted on to Norman. But it is not nearly so common to see a church in which Hellenism has been added to Victorianism and a touch of Romanesque thrown in afterwards, and the whole thing topped off with a Cubist roof. In Baltimore the waves have been very capricious, and a passionate desire to swim on the crest of each fashionable wave has played Old Harry with the finances of the faithful. For if a church has just completed, with the help of a first and second mortgage and perhaps a small bond issue, a magnificent House of Worship on the model of the Temple to Pallas Athene in Athens, it is naturally rather a tricky financial operation to go into the money-market within a month or two to raise funds to tear down and replace it with a Byzantine fane on the lines of the Mosque of the Holy Wisdom in Constantinople. In the days of the grand boom, the operation was, perhaps, just possible. But when Depression hit the country, it became utterly impossible, and the outskirts of Baltimore are littered with classical apses that only lack a roof, a nave, a chancel, and an aisle or two, and perhaps a west front, to make a very handsome church, or with lonely Romanesque basilicas that are sad reminders, probably, of the failure of a bond issue in the era of the Romanesque, or pre-Classical, wave.

But there is more art in Baltimore than is concealed in half-finished churches. There is, for instance, the staggering collection of the Walters family which has been presented to the City. It must have been the biggest private collection in the world, and it must contain more real, genuine, honest-to-God junk than any ten other private collections. Not that there is not some glorious stuff in it. The stained glass windows from the Cathedral at Sens, the ninth-century ivories, the alabaster figurines, the jewels, the enamels from Limoges, and scores of other treasures, are flawless masterpieces. But when Mr. Walters died, it was found that, in addition to his famous collection, there were still 243 unopened packing cases in the cellars, and then the junk began to tumble out. There are at present about a thousand pictures in the cellars for which there is no room in the galleries above. It would have taken a very long time even to glance at the entire thousand, but a random selection here and there gave me the impression that about one in seven was definitely interesting, that two of the other six were pleasant mediocrities, and that the rest would have made Landseer look like a genius. But even if all the junk was thrown aside — and, to judge from the learning and connoisseurship of the Curator and his assistants, it will be thrown aside pretty quickly and firmly — enough will be left to make the Walters Museum one of the most important in the United States.

There are many things to be recorded of Baltimore, and they have been recorded, without a doubt, in the books. There is, for instance, the quiet bourgeoise lady, Elizabeth Patterson, who brought down upon her head the whole wrath of the Great Emperor Napoleon himself because she married Lieutenant Jerome Bonaparte of the French Navy, and Jerome was required for a more important destiny. In fact the Kingdom of Westphalia was to be created especially for him, and the man who had himself taken a Creole to wife and crowned her Empress of the French, suddenly drew the line, rather illogically, at crowning a Baltimorean Queen of Westphalia.

Then there is the fox-hunting tradition of England which survives to this day in the many packs of hounds in Maryland. Outside Baltimore, the club-house of the Elkridge Harford Hounds is the relic of ancient Kennels, though I am bound to admit that after experiencing some of the characteristic hospitality of the neighbourhood I was uncertain whether it was foxes or elks which had been hunted in the old days, and whether I was expected to shout "Fore" or "Hark Forard" on the course itself. It was on this golf course that I first encountered the Southern Tact which is so famous all over the world. After I had played an unexpectedly skilful stroke with a niblick or what not, my caddie asked me, with a bland innocence, if I was a member of the British Walker Cup Team. That left nothing for me to do but to hand him a dollar without a word and proceed with the game.

In the Museum there is a portrait of Ross Winans who went from Baltimore long ago to work in Russia for the Tsars and came back to Baltimore again, and one of Thorowgood Smith, the second Mayor of the City, in all the glory of his own invented eye-glasses — two lenses dangling from a black silk ribbon tied round his forehead and a picture of the race-course at Pimlico, sudden echo of a small and squalid corner of London.

If you wander in the street markets you will find a mass of colour, piled up heaps of apples and melons and tomatoes and bananas and scarlet chillies and corn and persimmon-coloured gourds, as gay as the old tradition of the cavaliers, and if you go up the street of the ships captains on to the top of Federal Hill you will see on the one side as far as the island that Lee fortified and on the other to the enormous white buildings of the Mail Order store miles away to the inland. If you explore long enough you will find Fleet Street and Thames Street and Shakespeare Street, twisting along near each other, and beside the narrow Pothouse Alley there is an old grey stone building that must have given the name to the Alley, for it was once the coaching-inn on the road from Baltimore to the rich farming district of Belair, the road down which the grain-wagons came thundering to the sea and the waiting clippers.

In Miller's Restaurant you will find the gigantic oysters of Chesapeake Bay.

I had never seen any oyster to equal in size, even remotely, the Blue Point, the Chincoteague, the Georgia Island, but I was assured that this was just the beginning of the season and that they were diminutive fellows compared to the later varieties.

But the most romantic part to me at any rate, of Baltimore was the street down at the harbour, along the wharf. There were ships advertised to sail for the "Dismal Swamps, for Tolchester, Ocean City, and Rehoboth Beach" (what a beautiful combination of Rome, Modernity, and the Bible); for the "Eastern Shores of Maryland and Delaware"; for travel by Rock Creek Line to Fort Smallwood and Fairview Beach; for a "Moonlight Trip to Love Point Ferry" (and it would be a dullard who could not make progress with his lady on such a magical voyage to such a magical place) and to those enchanted rivers the Annamessex, the Potomac, the Rappahannock, the Patuxent, and — glory of glories — the Piankatank. What a name Piankatank! Probably some damned scholar can prove in a jiffy that it is the Indian word for Stinking-Bison Gulch or something of the sort, but to me, as I stood and watched the carts drawn by the gaily harnessed mules rattling up the wharves, the river Piankatank seemed the far-off edge of Atlantis or Lodore.

No wonder that Walt Whitman got excited when he thought about the place names of the Red Indians. Was there ever a lovelier name than Shenandoah or Missouri? They are almost the sole legacy of that unfortunate race. A hundred years ago they were lords of the prairie and the range. Now all that is left of them is a few arrowheads of jade and obsidian and carnelian and agate, and a large body of stories for the delight of schoolboys, and a handful of survivors on the Reservations and these lovely names, and nothing more.

When I read the name of the Piankatank River, I thought of Whitman's verse about the red aborigines, and though I am not going to pretend that I could recite it word for word as I stood there on the wharf, yet at least I remembered where to find it, and had enough energy to look it up when I got home:

The red aborigines,
Leaving natural breaths, sounds of rain and winds,
     calls as of birds and animals in the woods,
     syllabled to us for names:
Okonee, Koosa, Ottawa, Monongahela, Sauk, Natchez,
     Chattahoochee, Kaqueta, Oronoco,
Wabash, Miami, Saginaw, Chippewa, Oshkosh,
     Walla-Walla,
Leaving such to the States they melt, they depart,
     charging the water and the land with names.

Well, that is Baltimore as I saw it, the City of Maryland, the City of North and of South, of colour and laughter and sun and romance. As my train steamed out of the Pennsylvania Station, the sun was setting over Maryland in a splendour of black and gold, the heraldic colours of the family of Calvert.

CHAPTER SIX

They shall fully enjoy materialism and the sight of products,
    they shall enjoy the sight of beef, lumber, breadstuff's,
    of Chicago, the great city.

WALT WHITMAN

It was an old-standing resolution of mine that if ever I went to Chicago, I would not refer in speech, thought, or deed to the existence of gangsters and gun men. I would be the first citizen from Europe to refrain from making wan, feeble, near-witticisms about armoured cars and Al Capone, and in so refraining I would earn the everlasting gratitude of the inhabitants of the second city of the United States. For fourteen years or more the Chicagoans, whether in Chicago or in any other part of the world, have had to put up with the everlasting cackle of people asking, "Are the streets really swept with machine-gun fire every hour or two?" and "Is it true that everyone wears bullet proof waistcoats, even with evening-dress?" and "How is it that anyone survives at all?" so that by this time they may be excused a sigh when they see a European heave in sight over the horizon. For a European over the horizon means the same old catechism. Now the Chicagoan has a great command of good manners. With every excuse to slug his guest behind the ear, or sock him on the jaw, he controls himself, smiles as gaily as he can under the circumstances, and murmurs, "Oh, well, you know," or some such non-committal remark. The sort of thing he might have said, if his native courtesy had deserted him for a moment, was this: "Of course there have been murders. What can you expect when our Prohibitionists handed a thousand million dollars on a plate to be fought for by the lowest dregs of Ireland, the lowest dregs of southern Italy? That reminds me," he might go on, pensively. "Am I wrong in fancying that somehow or other I seem to have heard of a murder or two in old Ireland itself? And that the Mafia in Sicily and the Camorra in Naples have not pursued their activities entirely in white kid gloves? And is it completely safe in Germany to stand up and say how greatly you dislike the face of Herr Göring, or in Russia to express in public your heartfelt conviction that Comrade Stalin is a crook, a morphine-maniac, and a spy in the pay of the Grand Duke Cyril?" To all of which it is extremely difficult for the haughty European to find a reply.

There is no doubt that American films and Chicago newspapers have played their part in creating this idea that Wabash Avenue at its busiest hour is pretty much the same as a good average day's skirmishing in the Forest of the Argonne during the summer of 1918. But, whatever my European confrères had done, I was determined to ignore the lessons of the American film and the captions of the Chicago newspapers.

The Twentieth Century Express pulled out of the pitch-darkness of the Grand Central Station (for at last I found a train in the crypt of the mighty cathedral), across the Harlem and into the red glow of a sunset which made upper Manhattan look almost attractive, and rolled past factories, past engine-sheds in which rows of strong, black, electric locomotives stood waiting for work, past the huge squat silhouette of the Polo Ground, and so out towards the open country of New York State. Bridge after bridge spanned the river, all steel and each of a different pattern. On the river the little tugs hauled away for dear life and the barges, green, blue, red, yellow, threw their long shadows on the water as the sun crept downwards behind low wooded scarps on the western bank. The scarps on the other side rose into higher, rockier, more jagged edges, but on our side there were still factories, shipbuilding yards, piles of stacked timber, a warehouse or two, and once a power station whose four tall chimneys were very like the four chimneys of the Lot's Road Power Station on the Thames in London.

For mile after mile it was the same, the west bank changing in the twilight from one loveliness to another, the east from one hideousness to another. We passed close to raw red and yellow brick factories that had been built right out into the water as if in deliberate challenge to the Hudson River. It was as if the vandals had said, "We will not only ruin your bank, but we will ruin you as well." Sometimes the loathsome buildings would be varied with a nice little dump of rusty tins half in and half out of the water, and sometimes with rusty tins that were not even collected into a dump, but looked as if they had been sown by a sower who had some notion of amassing a million dollars by raising a crop of nourishing foods of fifty-seven different varieties in a single field. And sometimes, instead of being red and yellow, the factory would be black, and sometimes there were high gaunt frames of iron that may have been anything in the world for all I know.

But on the western bank there were no signs of human progress. The rocky, serrated cliff rose steadily and turned gradually into a high bluff, with a level silhouette against the sky, and the woods began again and grew denser and denser until they came at last right down to the river's edge and were reflected with a dark steady reflection in the shadowy water. The sun had gone down behind the bluff, but once or twice there must have been a narrow cleft in the steep hillside, for a shaft of gold suddenly struck the water for a moment and then vanished in the above-coloured twilight that was so quickly falling. The unrippled surfaces of the river and the bluff were now all the same colour, a pearly grey, or was it a ghostly blue, or a luminous mother-of-pearl, or oyster-shell or the colour of the feathers of a pigeon? I do not know. It was indescribable except that it was beautiful. It changed imperceptibly all the time. Along the level silhouette of the bluff, where the edge of the Earth faded into space, there was a faint line of pale yellow. A small yacht went slowly down the stream, and a five-masted barque lay at anchor. Here and there a solitary fisherman was snatching the last minutes of the day. Darkness closed in. The ghostly grey went into black, and the lights of diminutive lighthouses began to shine, and I went off in search of a cocktail. Half an hour later I went back to the Observation-Car. The moon was at the full and the blackness which had harried away the mother-of-pearl had been harried away in its turn, and the river was a sheet of silver. At last we had out-run our chimneys and tins, and the east bank was a mass of reeds on a flat marshy stretch of land. To the west, the moon shone upon ridge after ridge of wooded hills.

By the time we had finished dinner, the train was lying motionless, high up athwart the town of Albany. Below us were the lights and the street-cars and the automobiles and the neon-signs of the cinemas. In the station it was dark, and the outline of the huge, silent train against the stars was like a symbol of the Machine-Age above a clattering and chattering of mortals.

I woke up next morning to find that we were running along the shore of Lake Michigan, and in a moment we were passing the town of Gary, Indiana, and I could see that the new world has nothing to learn from the old world in the art of making a beautiful place hideous. The chimneys and the smoke and the buildings and the ghastliness, against the background of the Lake, are on the approved model.

Gary, I believe, is called after a steel-magnate named Judge Gary, and I presume the adjective "garish" is also from that derivation. And if it was originally coined to describe the town, or the Judge either for that matter, it has acquired an altogether erroneous mildness of meaning.

I could put a great many stronger meanings to the word, and yet fall short of my opinion of both.

We passed Gary without stopping — so at least we were spared something — and came to Chicago,

Alas for resolutions! Something always conspires to bring them to the ground. Mine went the way of the rest — not, I think, through any fault of mine, but rather through a combination of circumstances. I arrived in Chicago, repeating to myself over and over again, "There are no gangsters here, and even if there are, they are no concern of mine." It was a cold day. A northeast wind was blowing off the Lake and gusts of mist kept blowing in from that fresh-water ocean. I was not feeling very well after the concentrated hospitality of New York and Baltimore. I presented two of my letters of introduction and both of my prospective victims were away from home. (It occurs to me that perhaps, after the cruel description of a Chicago hostess by a distinguished English lady-novelist not so long ago, all hostesses in and around Chicago now make a point of leaving home when visiting authors arrive. They certainly have every justification for doing so, after that unfortunate display of manners.)

So there I was. Tired, jaded, alone in a gigantic city, cold, and with nothing more attractive to do than to play the game by my publishers and walk around the streets collecting material for this book. And there are few things so unattractive in this world except, of course, to the true-blue Englishman — as playing the game by anyone, especially a publisher. However there was nothing for it, so out I went after luncheon, and began.

It was an unfortunate experience. The afternoon grew colder, the mist grew thicker, and I grew wearier. Everyone seemed to be in a tremendous hurry, scuttling hither and thither like an industrious rabbit. By comparison New York was a city of loungers, of idle, strolling, dilettanti, taking the air on Fifth Avenue under the doctor's orders. The rushing and the jostling and the bustling in Chicago were quite bewildering. And there was the dust and the grime. From the soot-clouds and the smoke-palls of London it is a far cry to the steam-heated, electric-locomotived, clean atmosphere of Manhattan. But Chicago is at least a third of the way back to London. The grime is beastly and the noise is appalling. Standing in Wabash Avenue when the street-cars and the Elevated were in full swing, I felt that I had heard nothing like it since the old days of field-gun barrages. Fulton Street, Brooklyn, seemed in my recollection to be the sort of place where shepherds piped to their flocks, and the lambkins gambolled in the rustic scene. To make it worse, and more painfully realistic, the metal connections between the street-cars and their overhead wires were very faulty and there was an incessant spluttering of bangs and cracks, and an incessant flashing of blue flames in the air, as the hideous contraptions bell-clanged and wheel-screeched along. But I was resolved not to give in. Tired, nervous, cold, dusty, jerking into the air at each bang and cowering at each blue flame, nevertheless I kept on down Wabash Avenue with all the dogged tenacity of the sons of Britain, muttering to myself: "It's quite all right. It is not gangsters. It is only a street-car. Not gangsters at all. Only a street car."

It was about half-past five in the evening. Darkness had fallen, and the shops were shutting and the crowds in the street were greater than ever, and the people were moving faster than ever, the automobiles slower than ever. Suddenly I was pushed aside even more ruthlessly than usual. I turned to whimper a faint protest and saw that my jostler was a big, clean-shaven, iron-jawed policeman. He had just come out of a big Department Store and in his left hand he was carrying a sack, sealed and tied, and in his right a pistol that looked, to my fevered imagination, about the size of a medium-sized rifle. He was followed closely by a second policeman, also big, also clean-shaven, also iron-jawed, and he too carried what looked like a medium-sized rifle in each hand. Both were covered with cartridge-belts and bedecked with holsters. They strode across the sidewalk and jumped into an armoured-car that was cruising along slowly beside the curb. It was the last straw. I sprang into a taxi, drove back to the Palmer House, and locked myself into my room with a bottle of whisky and a small modicum of soda-water, and when I had drunk the lot I went to bed.

There are two separate and distinct parts of Chicago. One is Michigan Boulevard, and the other is all the rest The Boulevard is a truly magnificent street. The rest of Chicago is hideous. The Boulevard is broad, clean, spacious. The skyscrapers, though more ornate than the best of New York's, stand in a long, splendid line that almost rivals Manhattan, and cool dry breezes blow from Lake Michigan. The automobiles go bowling up and down in endless procession, and there is a feeling in the air of dignity and grandeur, coupled with a vast civic pride. I heard even a traffic policeman singing cheerfully to himself as he stood at his post. "Here is a street," you say as you look at Michigan Boulevard, "that is worthy of the second city of a great country, a city that is proud of itself, of its universities and its law schools, its parks and gardens, its libraries and its art galleries, its music and its schools of medicine, its museums and its aquarium and its planetarium and its science."

"Here," you say to yourself, "is a city that in a hundred years has acquired something of the civic spirit of Athens in the days of Pericles. Pheidias would not have despised it, nor would Aristotle have scorned to walk in its gardens."

That is Michigan Boulevard and all that it stands for. Now look at the other part of this, the second city of a great country. A few yards from the Boulevard, you plunge into narrow, dirty, noisy streets. Wabash Avenue and State Street are the best of them, and they are bad enough. But at least they are well-paved and well-lit at night. But if you go past them and push steadily south, that is to say parallel to the lake, and keep on bearing westerly, or inland, in a moment or two you are in dingy slums. The streets are full of holes; the houses are small, shabby, and sordid; the shops, miserable and uninviting. The atmosphere seems to give the impression that the drainage system is not what it might be, and at night the lamps are few and far between. It is possible to walk in two minutes from a brilliantly lit thoroughfare into a district of utter darkness, where there is hardly an automobile and where the few pedestrians seem to shuffle past furtively and in dread. These mean streets are seldom labelled with their names, and there is an utter absence of anything that could be remotely described as civic pride. The whole place looks like a disreputable alley-cat that only hopes that no one will pay any attention to it while it slinks from garbage-tin to garbage-tin. Further south, again, there is a long street called Prairie Avenue which might be a street in a town in Poland in the nineteenth century a year or two after a war has passed by. Here and there are solid, well-built houses, but the rest are small and decaying, and there are almost as many patches of open, unbuilt ground as there are houses. These empty spaces are covered with rank grass, weeds, old bricks, bottles, bits of derelict machinery, old fragments of corrugated iron, and, of course, the inevitable crop of rusty tins. Long, straggling grasses grow between the rough paving-stones of Prairie Avenue, in the second city of a great country, and wave forlornly in the light breezes. It is a dismal place.

Even more dismal, though at the other end of the social scale, is the northern end of Chicago. I drove out to it on a day of torrential rain. The first incident in this pilgrimage in this centre of commerce and hustle, was a seven-minute halt while a small boat went slowly down the Chicago River to the Lake, and the bridge was hoisted up to let it pass. There are, I think, eight bridges between Franklin Street and the Lake, and presumably the traffic at each of them was held up for seven minutes by this funny little boat. It was rather a busy time of the day, and before the bridge was down again there was a jam of motor-cars on the Boulevard that seemed to reach as far as the Stevens Hotel. I always thought that the level-crossings in the ancient City of Lincoln, in England, held the record for time-wasting, but Chicago has got Lincoln beaten hollow.

The next landmark was the Wrigley Building. The only thing that need be said about it is that it is not so ugly as the sight of a man or woman actually chewing the stuff. There is something about that monotonous champ, champ, champ, that painful working of the lower jaw, and that unwinking vacuity of expression which always seems to go with the habit, that fills the beholder with rage mingled with a certain admiration. The rage is because such ugliness as the face of a gum-chewer can exist in the world, and the admiration is for Mr. Wrigley who, when God has created Man in His own image, can so easily reduce him to the image of a cow. I saw an advertisement in a train in America — I cannot remember where — which ran as follows: "Wrigley's is the finishing touch to a good meal." And by Heavens! that advertisement is right. Wrigley's is the finishing touch to any meal, however good.

After the Wrigley Building we arrived at a really remarkable edifice. It was a tower, built of large, square, yellow stones, and designed with a hideousness that was almost frightening. It stood in the middle of the street, all by itself, and looked like a tower that had been built by a maniac with the express purpose in his loyal but befuddled mind of pleasing Queen Victoria. Had it been constructed of Scottish granite and decorated here and there with tartan, primroses, and a few stags antlers, that tower would have fitted tolerably well into the landscape around Balmoral Castle. I was told that it was the only building that survived the Great Fire of 1871, and could think of nothing to say except "Why?"

By the time we had got over the shock of this astonishing Tower, we were spinning through the beautiful Lincoln Park, and after that we came to a scene that was very characteristic of Chicago. On our left there were huge luxury hotels and blocks of apartments and big private houses, on our right an expanse of dismal mud-flats stretching to the Lake, luxury on one side and mud on the other.

But there is no mud-flat to mar the residential suburb of Evanston. Sheridan Road seems to run for miles between neat, stone, private houses, standing well back from the road and each one surrounded by trees. It is almost like a town in a forest. There must be thousands of these quietly solid houses, and the architecture of them is a positive triumph of imagination. For every single one is different in style to all the rest. Evanston is the exact antithesis of Guilford at Baltimore. Guilford was town-planned and built in general harmony with the Carroll house. Evanston has not been planned, and it is built in general harmony with nothing. It is a fine example of what the famous Rugged Individualism is really capable of when it gets among the Arts. And the extraordinary thing about the architecture of these Evanston houses is that although there must be about ten thousand separate and different specimens of how to build a private residence, not a single one is anything but ugly. In no single case has an architect, desperately searching round in his mind for a new and original pattern, happened to hit upon a beautiful one. It might have been thought that out of all those thousands, one might have been lovely by accident. But no. All are revolting.

The rain poured steadily down as we drove further and further into the heart of this architectural nightmare, and it became increasingly clear that residential Evanston is no stronger on drainage than some of those dark little streets in Chicago's slum-land. A small booklet entitled *Chicago Welcomes You* lays emphasis, among the many attractions of the city which the visitor ought not on any account to miss, upon the Drainage Canal in the neighbourhood. I saw few signs of the results of its work. As the afternoon advanced, the roads were dotted with huge puddles of standing water, and any small slope was like a river, while the football-grounds and lawn-tennis courts of North-Western University were under water.

Very few cities have ever had such an opportunity for creating a masterpiece of the art of Town-Planning as Chicago. The Fire gave the City Fathers a clean sheet on which to work, and the unique advantage of the site, being the natural junction of the railroads and the lake-borne traffic, soon provided fabulous wealth for the rebuilding. Yet, in spite of these gifts, the business was sadly bungled and all that Chicago can show of magnificence is a single street. The rest is melancholy.

There was one place in which I found a meeting of the two different spirits of Chicago, the proud spirit of Civic Responsibility and the spirit of the dismal rest. Curiously enough they met in a Municipal Police-Court.

As I wanted to see American Justice in action, I penetrated into the press-room of the Police-Court and introduced myself as a London journalist. The room was exactly as it appears in Hecht and MacArthur's play *The Front Page*. Half a dozen telephones, walls scrawled over with pencilled obscenities and crude drawings, a couple of plain tables, a few chairs, a poker-game with an old crumpled pack of cards, a man in shirt-sleeves reading a newspaper, and an unceasing flow of blasphemy, these were the principal ingredients in the scene. A young reporter at once offered to get me a place beside the Judge in any court I liked, and, sure enough, in about three minutes he had haled me up to a Judge on his Bench, and, to my alarm, leant over and attracted the attention of the great man by tweaking his sleeve in the middle of a speech by an attorney. I expected a sharp sentence for Contempt of Court for both of us, but the Judge turned round, shook me by the hand, said he was glad to know me, and that he would be pleased if I made myself at home on the Bench for as long as I liked. Meanwhile the attorney went on thundering unheeded.

The procedure of the Court was very informal. As each case was called, the witnesses, the defendant, and the defendant's counsel, came forward and grouped themselves casually in front of the Bench. It was usually quite impossible to tell which was which, though it was a pretty safe bet that the most shifty-looking of the party would turn out to be the defendant's attorney. The police witness, usually a big, good-looking youth in a smart blue uniform with brass buttons, and a spotlessly clean blue shirt and black tie, gave his story first, and then the fun would start. The defending attorney would begin an elaborate series of technical objections, would usually be interrupted by his own client, who would be passionately contradicted by one of his own witnesses. Then they would all start shouting together and quarrelling bitterly among themselves. All this time Judge X would sit in his big chair and look at them and say nothing. Then suddenly he would ask a question that brought everybody up short, and in a few minutes he had everything neatly unravelled, a sentence delivered, and the whole case finished. The party in front of the bench would disappear, except for the defending attorney who would be left alone, shouting appeals for clemency, protests against injustice, and accusations of corrupt evidence. During this stentorian interlude Judge X would be busy recording his decision upon his calendar, and then he would look up and say "Go away" in tones of such deadly quietness that the bluster would suddenly evaporate and the attorney would retreat in haste.

And so it went on all through the morning. There was no delay between the cases. Men were charged with being in possession of guns, of trading in dope, of owning illegal slot-machines, of failing to pay rent, or stealing, of assault and battery, of every conceivable sort of minor villainy, and to each and all Judge X listened and listened and listened while he gazed steadily at them. A woman explained that her husband, who had been subpoenaed in a case, could not attend the Court as he had got a nice lucrative job for the day.

"Then tell him from me," said the Judge in a gentler tone than ever, "that if he is not here to-morrow at 9.30 A.M., it will be just too bad for him."

An elderly man was found guilty of some petty misdemeanour and sentenced to five dollars fine and five dollars costs. With a heavy sigh he picked up a crutch and stumbled heavily out of the Court. Judge X turned to the police sergeant and said, "Has that man got a wooden leg?"

"Yes, Judge." "I think we've been a little hard on him. Shall we make it two and two?"

"Make it one and one, Judge," said the sergeant, and the Judge nodded.

A flashily dressed youth was charged with stealing a fire-extinguisher and was found guilty on the clearest possible evidence. His own story was a mass of contradictions and absurdities, and the District Attorney had no trouble in demolishing it. The sentence was thirty days in the House of Correction, and the defending lawyer exploded into a tornado of protest. Waving a half-smoked cigar in the Judge's face, he launched into an eloquent appeal for clemency. "Thirty days", "first offence", "just married", "give the boy a chance", "blasting a young life", were the themes on which he played his noisy variations, and the Court-room rang with his moral indignation. Judge

X waited patiently until at last the harangue was over, and then he replied: "If you had advised your client to tell the truth, he would have been put on Probation. I am not sentencing him for a stupid little theft. I am sentencing him because he has forsworn his oath." He then turned to the youth and delivered a simple and moving little speech on the sanctity of an oath sworn in Court upon the Bible, and then the next case was called and the procession of battered wrecks, dope-addicts, brutal hooligans, sub-human Africans, smart young embryonic gangsters, sneak-thieves, petty racketeers, drunkards, and sweepings of a vast, cosmopolitan city, started again on its dismal journey.

As I walked home to my hotel, I saw a large advertisement on a board which stated that Judge X was running for re-election as Judge on November 6th, and I reflected upon the strange system which makes a wise and humane Judge dependent upon the votes of, presumably, the very sort of scum and dregs of mankind that had been passing before him that morning.

In the evening I visited a Music Hall in the Loop and saw a Russian propaganda film, which proved beyond shadow of doubt that the Five Years Plan was bound to succeed, that Stalin was the greatest man in the world, and that Individualism and Capitalism were utterly doomed. At the end of the film the orchestra played the lovely old tune "Maryland," which has been taken by the British Labour Party and re-labelled "The Red Flag." As I sat in that theatre in the heart of the greatest capitalist country in the world, I could not help recalling the rather unfortunate verses which a perfervid British revolutionary wrote for "The Red Flag" on the top of a bus in a London traffic jam, and the stirring lines in which he proclaims:

Look round: the Frenchman loves its blaze,
The sturdy German chants its praise,
In Moscow's vault its hymns are sung,
Chicago swells the surging throng.

The Great Exhibition (called for some reason, perhaps as a delicate if rather belated compliment to the Marquis de Lafayette, the Exposition) of a Century of Progress was just coming to an end, but I kept my oath and did not go to it. I always had an excuse ready. Once it was a famous English novelist who was passing through Chicago on her way to lecture in Mason City, Iowa (the Mason Citizens had "purchased" her for an hour and a half, as her lecture agent so gracefully put it in a letter), and we sauntered along the Lake and discussed our hosts. And once it was a young American Novelist with whom I sat upon a tall stool for many an hour and listened to the story

70

of Mayor Cermak, the "Martyr," who had been elected to clean up the City after Big Bill Thompson had been busting King George V on the snoot, and the peculiar circumstances surrounding the purchase by Chicago of its forest-parks. So what with one thing and another, I never got to the Exposition. But to judge from this extract from the *Chicago Tribune* which describes the scene in the grounds on the last day, it would appear that, whatever else may have progressed in the last century, it is not Human Nature:

"The riotous merrymakers took possession of the $48,000,000 playground, drank everything in sight except the lake, and snatched everything movable as souvenirs. It was a vicious mob-spectacle; men, women and children crushed into unconsciousness, battling police platoons whipped back by souvenir hunters in on the 'kill,' hospital ambulances screaming through the packed streets.

"Thrifty housewives, their children clutching frantically to their coats, uprooted rare plants and shrubbery and trudged off triumphantly with their $200 bargain — bought with a fifty-cent piece for admission. The $500,000 horticultural building was almost denuded.

"If a sign remains along the eighty-three miles of streets and concessions, thank faulty eyesight and the scarcity of ladders. The street of villages, joy of the 1934 Exposition, was sacked."

There are also, I believe, some Stock Yards in Chicago. I did not visit them, but I was informed of their existence. Frequently.

CHAPTER SEVEN

O the farmer's joys!
Ohioan's, Illinoisian's, Wisconsinese', Kanadian's, Iowan's,
     Kansian's, Missourian's, Oregonese' joys!
To rise at peep of day and pass forth nimbly to work,
To plough land in the fall for winter-sown crops,
To plough land in the spring for maize,
To train orchards, to graft the trees, to gather apples in the fall.

WALT WHITMAN

There are two main routes from Chicago to the west for the British traveller. The first, and by far the commonest, is by the Union Pacific direct to San Francisco. The second is over the Northern Pacific via Minneapolis to Seattle and Portland. I therefore decided to take neither, but to dodge about the country between the two. Never having heard of any Englishman who has visited Omaha, save only the wandering lecturer who sees nothing on his bewildering rushes to and fro but a sleeping-berth, a luncheon table, and an ocean of faces, I decided to make that city my first stopping-place west of Chicago. There was also another reason for visiting Omaha, a childish one both in the literal and in the metaphorical sense of the word. Ever since I was old enough to read the romances of Mr. G. A. Henty and such stories as *Fifty-two Tales of Wild Life East and West*, I had had a mysterious and inexplicable desire to visit Sioux City and Council Bluffs. For years I pored over the rather indifferent map of the United States with which we were provided at school, and rolled the romantic names round my infantile tongue, Rio Grande del Norte and Sacramento and Great Falls and Savannah and a hundred others; but I always came back to Sioux City and Council Bluffs, with Cheyenne a good third. On this journey to America there was not time to visit more than one of them — already I was beginning to get some notion into my head that America is a tolerably large place and I therefore chose Council Bluffs as the most convenient for subsequent journeyings.

It was early morning when the Pullman attendant woke me up, and I peered eagerly out through a thin grey mist. To anyone else there was not much to see. Brown cliffs rising up from the bed of the Missouri River, crowned with small straggly willows, or they may have been birches or ash or aspen for all I know, and nowhere higher than perhaps a hundred feet. That was all. But to me it was a flying carpet that took me back to happy days long ago with wigwams and tomahawks and cowboy-hats and lariats, deadly ambushes and chivalric rescues, wild gallops on wooden mustangs and vast slaughterings of bison that must have seemed to our poor dull-witted elders to be only logs of wood from the wood-shed. And there was a day of days, supremest of all days in that desperate frontier warfare which swayed from the artichoke-bed to the laurel-bushes, from the laburnum shrubbery round by the guelder-roses to the stable-yard, when Buffalo Bill himself came to our suburb with his real cowboys and his real redskins, whooping, galloping, firing Winchester repeaters from the hip, lassoing, picking up handkerchiefs from the ground while riding at full speed, and swinging down behind the tearing horse so that the rider was invisible to the lurking marksman. I gazed in ecstasy through the blurred window and the long-ago Past came back to me.

Surely that was a gleam of bright feathers among the trees on Council Bluffs and another, and another. Feathered head-dresses of the War-Path, and a shaft of early-morning sun upon the head of a tomahawk, and a settler's log-cabin, peaceful and unsuspecting, upon the edge of the Bluffs... . The colours dancing in and out... . The raiding-party converging upon the doomed cabin... . Massacre and torture. Death at the stake... . But listen... . A great shout, and a thunder of hooves, and a cloud of dust, and the cowboys galloping to the rescue with Colonel Cody himself at their head, firing a Colt revolver from each hip. The log-cabin is saved. The redskins disappear. Everything disappears except the brown wall of the Bluffs and the stumpy trees, and there is a grinding of brakes and we have arrived at Omaha.

Omaha is a large, cheerful, modern town. The streets are wide, and the buildings plain, solid, of a reasonably low altitude. The people are either busy or anxious to be busy. There are no idle rich, for the simple reason that no one who was rich enough to be idle would live of his own free will in Omaha. It is a commercial city and nothing else, pleasant enough and unsophisticated enough, but making no sort of claim to be a centre of Culture or a Beauty Spot or a Health Resort. As in Chicago, the pride of Omaha is the Stock Yards. But for the wandering traveller there is a big difference between the two. In Chicago you expect that everyone will try to drag you out to see the Yards, and you are prepared accordingly with all the lying excuses and side-stepping evasions which are so essentially part of the old-world, courteous *politesse* of Europe. As a result you can visit Chicago and blandly baffle every effort to bully, entice, or kidnap you to an inspection of the meat-packing establishments of Messrs. Armour and the rest of them. But at Omaha I was caught off my guard. I had not known that Omaha possessed the second biggest Stock Yards of the world, beating Kansas City by a short head (of cattle, presumably), and I was taken unawares, and in a moment I was being whisked off to see them. I tried very hard to shut ears, eyes and nose, but even so I carried away a few vivid, too vivid, impressions.

There was the vastness of them and the countless miles of railway sidings. There was the perpetual swirl of smoke, whether from the locomotives or from the furnace that boiled down the by-products I did not enquire. There was the picturesque-ness of the men on horses who marshalled the cattle into the pens far below — I was watching from the top of a high office building and looking straight down into the Yards. There was the sudden opening of an elevator inside the office building and the eruption from it of twelve gigantic young men in open-necked flannel shirts, riding breeches, big, muddy boots, and Stetson-hats, and all carrying riding-whips, and all looking rather less intelligent, and much more bewildered at the novelty of their surroundings, than a troupe of sea-lions in a circus-tent. And lastly, firstly, all the time, all-pervading, inescapable, there was the Smell.

I retreated from the Stock Yards as soon as I could, and congratulated myself even more heartily than before upon my tactics in Chicago, and made a note in red ink in my diary: "Kansas City, third largest Stock Yards in the world. Mem. Avoid Kansas City."

The residential districts of Omaha are unfortunately reminiscent of Evanston in the individuality of the architecture. There is this difference, however. In Omaha about one house in three hundred is built on the Colonial model and is beautiful.

There is one building of considerable interest in Omaha. It is the Art Gallery, presented to the City by a rich lady. It is a large, square, imposing building, made of grey stone and built on a simple, modern, dignified design. It was, in fact, one of the most attractive modern buildings which I saw west of the Atlantic Coast. But as an Art Gallery it had, at any rate up to the time of my visit, a fatal defect. It contained no Art. The benefactress who built it presumably expended all her energies and available cash on the Gallery and left it to other ladies and gentlemen to cover the walls and fill the niches. So far no one had come forward, and the only exhibits were the works of contemporary local talent. Without doubt benefactions will be forthcoming in time. A hot-dog magnate or toothpaste millionaire may even now be lurking in Omaha who will shower Rembrandts, Van Dycks, Cellinis, and Michaelangelos, upon his home town. In the meanwhile, would it not be a graceful act if the ancient City of Baltimore lent some of its huge surplus from the Walters collection to its newer sister in the Middle West? There will never be room in Baltimore for the contents of those two hundred and forty-three packing-cases that were found unopened in the cellar. And even if Baltimore did not lend any of her first-rank works of art, there are plenty of second-rank pieces which she could easily spare for a few years, until the local millionaire weighs in. "What concern is it of yours, you interfering Britisher?" cries the indignant Baltimorean at this point. He thinks he has got me cornered. But I have a very cunning defence. "None whatever," I reply, and he goes away, with a baffled look in his eye and writes an indignant letter to the *Sun* newspaper, complaining about meddling travellers. On the other hand, I shall probably be appointed Honorary Inspector of the Stockyards in Omaha, or Captain in the Nebraskan Marine Artillery, and it will be the old Swings and Roundabouts story again.

Another striking feature of Omaha is, or rather was — it may all be changed by now — the Drink Laws. When I arrived, it was illegal to buy hard liquor in Nebraska, and it was impossible to buy whisky or gin in more than five out of every six cafés and restaurants; and certainly not more than two in every six advertised the excellence and purity of their spirits. In order to evade this hideous restriction upon the liberties of the individual, certain of the Citizenry of Omaha had formed themselves into a club, with premises on the first floor of the Hotel Fontenelle, for the purpose of buying one another an occasional high-ball. The principle was sound, and the execution of it admirable, for the club was comfortable and handsome. There were, however, two drawbacks to it. Firstly, it was called, in Old Englyshe letters, the Mayfair, which was, to say the least of it, incongruous in the Middle West. I tried hard to hope that the Fontenelle was named for Bernard Le Bovier de F., the French writer who died at the age of a hundred in 1757, and that Mayfair was perhaps a Middle Western corruption of Marivaux or, even, better still, Molière. But I am afraid it was a forlorn hope. The second drawback to the club was that on the ground floor of the hotel there was a wide-open bar at which the same drinks could be bought at a smaller cost and without a yearly subscription. Furthermore, if the client of this bar so desired it, he could be served by a fetching damsel, dressed in the costume of an English hunting-squire. It was not until I had been in Omaha for two days that I discovered this bar, and as it had only been open for a month, the Mayfair clubmen had not yet heard of it.

In the club there was a superb negro singer, as splendid as any, after Robeson, that I have heard. He was singing in clubs and restaurants in order to save up money to finish his Course of Music at Tuskegee and start as a composer. We talked long and late one night. But when he said mournfully, "Our two races just misunderstand each other," I had not the courage to ask him what he thought of the White.

But I had not gone to Omaha to see Omaha, pleasant city though it is. I had gone to catch a glimpse of the famous Middle West, that valley of the Mississippi River that is thirteen hundred miles long and six or seven hundred miles wide. This Middle West has long been the bogey of Europe. If the United States Senate refused to ratify a treaty, we always ascribed it to pressure from the Middle West; if a new and super-efficient tractor began to undercut British tractors, it was always due to the mass-production that was possible only on the illimitable Middle West; if Europe was flooded with abominably bad cinema pictures, it was because they were specially designed for the hicks of the Middle West; if the United States wanted its war-debt repaid, it was owing to the ignorant clamour, we explained to each other, of the citizens of the Middle West who were so unreasonable as to want their money back. In fact, we made the Middle West into a sort of Colossus, alternately illiterate and politically acute, alternately half-witted and shrewd, alternately turning its back and its telescope upon European affairs, alternately wrapped in a loutish sleep and possessed of demoniac vigilance.

I motored out of Omaha with a friend to see something of this enigmatic land. We drove out by a curly, twisty road that was very unlike the great highroads that I had seen so far in the country. But its twistiness was historical, like that of so many English roads, for it had once been the only trail westwards out of Omaha, and in the days when that trail was first trodden by white men, it was more important to twist and curl under the skyline than to march arrogantly over hill and dale in full view of lurking marauders. One of the first villages we came to was called Elk City, and a huge notice-board on the outskirts announced its name and added, with a very proper civic pride, "Population 42." The sign-painter of Elk City must be a busy man, for even in a community of that inconsiderable size, there must be births and deaths and departure of old citizens and arrival of new. In time the march of Progress will dispossess that homely craftsman, and a machine will click up the ever-increasing numbers as Elk City soars to the hundred, and then to the glorious thousand, mark.

The road was lined with notices imploring the electorate to realize before it was too late that the safety and welfare of the entire Union depended upon the election of Mr. O. Boye to the post of Assistant Surveyor of Sidewalk Paving, or of Mr. Cyrus Hotcha to the high office of Deputy Clerk to the

Inspector of Inland Waterways. For in the United States, it appears, elections are real elections. There is none of your dull, niggardly British system of electing one man or woman, out of three or four candidates, to be a Member of Parliament and then, having elected the Member, for getting his, or her, face, opinions, election-pledges, political creed, forgetting even his, or her, name, — nay more, forgetting his, or her, very existence for the next four or five years. There is more fun in an American election, for on the very same day the elector has a chance of choosing his Senator, his Judge, his Sheriff, and, indeed, pretty nearly everything down to Postman, Pullman-car Conductor, and Assistant-Polishers-of-the-Cuspidors in the State Legislature. Thus the traveller has the diversion of reading by the wayside that Mr. Q. Z. Jugg will, if elected to the office of Sub-Inspector of the Main Sewer, sub-inspect the Main Sewer more conscientiously, and with a more incorruptible impartiality, than it has ever been sub-inspected before in all the long proud story of Nebraskan Sewerage.

The sun shone gaily as we bowled along between these rows of appeals and exhortations, and, as we drew further and further away from Omaha, we were able to catch a glimpse or two of the countryside, and at last we got entirely clear of the elections and were able to stop the car and have a look at the Nebraskan plains that lay before us in the sunlight. The country was not unlike the Somme country of France. There were the same gentle slopes and rolls of ground, the same dotted farm-houses, and the same wooded valleys. The difference was a difference of colour, for Picardy is white with chalk and its green is a dusty, chalky green, whereas Nebraska is black with the blackness of its soil, and its green is dark and rich, except where the winter wheat makes a lighter splash of colour. A great drought had just come to an end, and the landscape was chequered, light and dark, with the deep colour of the alfalfa crop and the brassy fields of corn that had been so scorched by the endless sun of spring, summer and early fall that they were not worth the trouble of harvesting. In the distance the blue of the Elkhorn River made a cheerful patch between its tree-covered banks with their oaks and lindens and walnuts, and here and there a cluster of cottonwoods added an almost Scandinavian touch of flaxen gold against the Elkhorn's blue. Far away, beyond the river, Nebraska stretched to the horizon and for many a hundred miles beyond the horizon.

Our objective, a farm-house, was nearer at hand. It was a neat white building, with green shutters, of course, and a quantity of outhouses, and a clump of trees round about. It was forty miles from a city of no outstanding size, and entirely isolated from village, hamlet, or even neighbouring farm, and yet it was equipped with electric light, refrigerator, central heating, and telephone. What percentage of the farms within forty miles of London, the biggest city in the world, have any of those amenities, let alone all four of them? I only point that out in passing in order to annoy my patriotic fellow-countrymen for, personally, I do not care two straws what electrical equipment the farms of England, or anywhere else, possess or lack. Agriculture has never been a passion in my life.

I was, therefore, rather at a disadvantage in listening to the agricultural talk of the farmer who greeted us as we alighted from the car. At times, even with the best will in the world to lower his talk to the standard of two poor townees, Mr. Johansen became alarmingly technical. But in spite of my ignorance, and Mr. Johansen's professional erudition, I learned some interesting things not about farming, but about the mysterious, Sphinx-like Middle West.

We went all over the farm, all the eight hundred acres of it, and a quaint trio we must have looked. My friend, an Omahan banker, neat and dapper in his banking suit; I, as near to neatness and dapperness as I can ever contrive to get; and Mr. Johansen, huge, fair-haired, blue-eyed, young, slouching, in rough farm-clothes, slow of speech and quick to laughter. We set out, the townees picking their way delicately in exquisite shoe, the countryman striding along unconscious of mud or slush. We saw the fat young calves that had come in that week from the Great Sandhills — up Wyoming way — to be fattened for the Stock Yards. The calves had come from a ranch 350 miles away. With the strains of "Git along, little dogies" to which I had been dancing a night or two before, in my ears, I asked how many weeks it took to drive cattle 350 miles, in these days when the roads are jammed with traffic. "I started on a Monday morning in my automobile," said Mr. Johansen, "and I got to the ranch that day. On Tuesday I selected my calves, and I got back on Wednesday just in time to get ready for them when they arrived in trucks."

It was several minutes before I tried any more of the taking-an-intelligent-interest stuff, and I gazed in prudently silent admiration at the chestnut-coloured son of the greatest Belgian stallion that ever came to America, and at the herds of cattle that were feeding at the corn-troughs while all the flies in Nebraska buzzed about trying to get the sugar out of the corn-canes. Then we got into Mr. Johansen's automobile and drove across the farm-lands to see fat sheep that were pasturing in a wooded dell beside a stream; a group of grandchildren of the Belgian stallion; an outhouse filled with up-to-date machinery; a group of men digging a well; and barns that were so bulging with corn that the boarding of the walls was bending outwards and a brick in the foundations had been dislodged by the pressure.

"Hey!" cried my Omahan companion, as he saw the sagging walls, "What's all this? What's all this?"

"Corn," replied Mr. Johansen, with a sort of paternal simplicity, as one speaks to an inquisitive baby.

"I know it's corn," answered the city man with some asperity. "But what is going to happen to that building if a high wind gets up?"

"Oh, it won't get up," said Mr. Johansen easily.

My friend was not so simply put off as all that. "But what will happen if it does?" he persisted.

"It will be all right," said Mr. Johansen with a big guffaw. "Some other part of Nebraska will get my corn, that's all. They'll gain what I lose."

From the expression of melancholy that settled upon my companion's face at this answer, I could almost deduce that his bank might have some financial interest in Mr. Johansen's corn remaining upon Mr. Johansen's land rather than upon some other portion of the Nebraskan plain, but I discreetly did not enquire. Anyway the thought did not diminish Mr. Johansen's joviality, and he pulled his car off the track and drove it slap across a field so that I should see at close quarters the little purple flower which we call, I believe, Lucerne in Britain, but they call Alfalfa. Thence he steered briskly up a dried river-bed, shouting gaily that if we stuck in the sand we could always get a tractor to pull us out. That crisis did not arise, however, and we emerged on to a field that was completely bare. "This," said Mr. Johansen with some solemnity, "is my most important field. It is here that I am paid by the Government to raise nothing at all. That is called National Recovery."

This, of course, brought us to those two great conversational topics, Depression and the New Deal. Mr. Johansen had a lot to say about both of them and about a third that was mainly confined to the Middle West, the Long Drought.

"They come here," said Mr. Johansen, "and they offer me money not to do this, and they offer me money not to raise that, so I take their money. Naturally I take it. Why not? Anybody would. But I could get through the Depression without it. I'm not going bankrupt so long as I'm farming a Nebraskan farm."

"Plenty of banks have gone bankrupt," said my companion gloomily. "Seven hundred out of thirteen hundred in Nebraska alone."

"And a good job too," cried Mr. Johansen gaily, striking the banker an ox-felling blow on the back. "We are getting down to reasonable farm-finance at last. Why, in the good old days before Depression, we could mortgage our farms as wildly as we pleased, because we knew perfectly well that our next year's profits would be so enormous that we could probably pay the whole mortgage off in a year. We're more careful now, and when we do borrow, we borrow from the Federal Land Bank. Government long-term credits, my boy.

That's the racket now." I thought, though I may have been mistaken, that my companion winced a little at the application of the word "racket" to anything so sacrosanct as the principles of banking.

"And I'll tell you another thing," went on Mr. Johansen. "Depression has made us more careful. We don't any longer leave our agricultural machinery lying out all winter. We put it away and oil it and use it again next year.

"And I'll tell you another thing," said Mr. Johansen. "Depression has finished all the get-rich-quick notions that we used to have. When I was a kid, we used to arrange our futures very simply. Get over college and then make a million dollars. That was all."

"What college were you at?" I enquired timidly. That, at least, was a safe un-agricultural question.

"Yale," said the farmer. "But that million-dollar stuff is finished. It's all small profits now, but steady ones. We've got to get accustomed to the English way, of choosing a trade and sticking to it for life. In the old days we went into farming as a nice outdoor occupation for a few years while we made a fortune on the stock-market. Now we're in it and we've got to stay in it, so we're learning our job at last."

"What about the Drought?" I asked.

"Well, the Drought was bad," said Mr. Johansen. "It was very bad. It burnt up the corn terribly. And it did more than burn the corn. We've had droughts before, but never such a long one. Other droughts have been bad on one or two crops, but this one was so long that it was bad for all the crops. But it had a good side too. We had to sit down and think out ways of dodging it, new farming methods, new crops, new ideas. I've learnt more about farming during the last year than in all my life before,"

"What will happen if you get another drought next year?" asked my companion.

"It will be bad, very bad," said Mr. Johansen. "But even another drought won't break us. Even N.R.A. can't break us. Look at that." And he swung his long arm in the direction of a hillside. "The longest drought on record, and look at that. After a few days rain, the winter wheat is up, and Strong as you like." He swung his arm on a wider circle, embracing this time not his own 800 acres but the whole Nebraskan plain, or, wider still, the whole of the Middle West. "The valley of the Missouri River," he exclaimed, "is the richest in the world. Seventy-five years ago it was nothing but grass and saplings and bands of Indians. Look at the corn-lands now, and the cattle, and the farm-buildings. Not a thing more than seventy-five years old. Do you think you can get that down with a silly little drought or two? Never. Your city-folk may talk of bankruptcies and ruin. Come and live on Nebraskan soil and learn what Nature can do in the way of recovery after a hard time. Nothing will worry you then.

"If you keep close to Nature," said Mr. Johansen, "you can't go wrong. Not in Nebraska anyway. Of course if you like to plough up your cattle-ranges and try to grow wheat as they did in South Dakota when wheat went to $2.20 a bushel during the War, then you deserve anything you get."

I asked what they did get.

"They got blown away," replied the farmer with a huge grin. "Yes, sir. There wasn't grass any more to hold their thin top-soil together and it got blown away. The last that was seen of it was a great dust-cloud over Baltimore and then it went out into the Atlantic." He laughed cheerfully at the notion, and from what I saw of the spirits of the Baltimoreans I imagine that they too must have laughed cheerfully at the flying farms of South Dakota.

A herd of Hereford cattle came past, fat and sleek and healthy. "There's a link with old England," said the farmer. "Herefords. Best cattle in the world for us. Your Scotch Angus are good, but they're terribly wild. Talking of Scotch …"

The sun was setting over the Elkhorn River as we drove home along the old trail, and the population of Elk City was still 42. Purple clouds were trailing over the Nebraskan plains, and lights were beginning to shine in the windows of the lonely farms.

I learnt a lot of things that afternoon, besides such important agricultural facts as that you can bury your silage in Nebraska, whereas in Iowa and Kansas you have to put it into towers. (Whether or not I shall ever find myself in Nebraska with a lot of silage on my hands, is a matter of some dubiety. The odds, I should say, were against it. But if the long shot came off, I should know exactly what to do with it. I should bury it without the slightest hesitation, although I must admit that what you do with it afterwards remains a dark mystery.)

As I say, I learnt a lot more than that, and found the answers to one or two of our European puzzles. For one thing I found that the Middle West is a long way from Europe. Even I, a European, felt incredibly remote as I stood on the banks of the Elkhorn River that afternoon. I was ten thousand miles further away than when I was in New York or Chicago, further away even than when I reached, later on, San Francisco. The whole outer world fades away. Nothing seems to be of any importance except the spring sowing or the fattening of cattle. What does it matter to you, as you stroll in the shadow of the cottonwoods, what the people of Memel think of the people in Lithuania? Would you leave your sheep beside the Elkhorn to go and fight for

Latvia against Poland? Would you lie awake at night in your Nebraskan farm, worrying about the justice of awarding Eupen and Malmédy to Belgium?

What have wars, thousands of miles away, to do with this peaceful, eternal, business of living on the soil, by the soil, for the soil? I used to think, as many others think, that the Middle West is supremely ignorant. I was wrong. The Middle West is supremely wise. It goes on its way, hating no man and fearing no man and saying, as Shakespeare's Corin said, "The greatest of my pride is to see my ewes graze and my lambs suck."

It knows very little about Europe, even though so many thousands of the farmers are first generation immigrants from Scandinavia, and many thousands more are children of first generation immigrants. "My father was born in Copenhagen," said Mr. Johansen, "but I am an American."

The Mississippi Valley takes them and makes them into Americans, because the Mississippi Valley is America. The cities of the East and of the long Pacific slope are important, but they are not the heart of the country. They talk more, but they mean less. They travel the world and broaden their minds, but when the ill-winds begin to blow it is not the East and West that stand unshakable. It is that Valley in the Middle that cannot be conquered.

CHAPTER EIGHT

From far Dakota's canons,
Lands of the wild ravine, the dusky Sioux, the lonesome
stretch, the silence,
Haply to-day a mournful wail, haply a trumpet-note for heroes.

WALT WHITMAN

My attempt to cut away from the standard routes of the European visitor was very nearly frustrated. From Omaha I had planned to leave the ordinary Chicago to San Francisco line at Lincoln, Nebraska, and strike north-westerly on the Chicago, Burlington and Quincy railroad into the State of Montana. Whether it was sheer carelessness, or whether it was subconscious pressure from the spirits of the myriad Britons who have passed that way, is a problem that may never be solved, but at any rate at Lincoln (the Capitol of which, incidentally, is a very splendid bit of modern American architecture) I installed myself in the dining-car of the San Francisco train instead of the Montana train and ordered a drink. As the Montana train was not due to leave for fifty minutes, I was puzzled when we started off in five, and as we rapidly gathered way and plunged forward into the night, I began to get exceedingly alarmed. Everything I possessed, except the clothes I was wearing was in the Montana train. Hasty enquiries soon showed that my greatest alarms were entirely justified, and I was off to San Francisco. But I need not have worried overmuch. Waiters, attendants, conductors, ticket inspectors, and other functionaries began leaping hither and thither, passing words to and fro, and within half a minute the express had halted and the door was unlocked for my escape. I threw a dollar-note to the waiter for my drink and hopped out into the darkness. The ticket collector leant out and waved and said, "We can't let you English visitors get a wrong idea of our railroads, sir."

I ran stumblingly back to the station and as I ran I wondered what would happen to an American who got, by mistake, into the Flying Scotsman at

King's Cross Station. At least I didn't really wonder, for I knew perfectly well that unless he cared to stop the train himself by pulling the cord and paying his five pounds, he would not be decanted until he reached the first halt, which is the Waverley Station of Edinburgh, about four hundred miles away.

The next day was my first whole day in an American train. We ambled on and on across the dreary waste of the north-western edge of Nebraska, and southerly edge of South Dakota. The country was very like our own Highland moors without the heather. Rolling hills stretched away on each side of the track. In Scotland they would have been purple with an occasional splash of green. In South Dakota they were yellow with short grass and yellow with sand. Even on the very rare patches of riper vegetation the weeds were a dusty green, like the leaves of an olive-tree, and they were spotted with tufts of sagebrush, cocked up in the air like the tails of innumerable rabbits that had been struck into immobility by an attack of jaundice. The far horizon was decorated with lines of unhappy, struggling fir-trees, which only seemed to be green because of the desolation of yellow sand and sage. For miles and miles and miles there was no human habitation in sight, and no sheep or cow or living thing except, sometimes, a flapping crow.

The place-names reflected the increasing, deepening despair of the old pioneers as they struggled painfully into the wilderness. They obviously started out full of hope and optimism, and the first names west of Lincoln are gay, jolly ones — Emerald, Pleasant Dale, Ruby, Aurora, Grand Island, Ravenna, Sweetwater, these are the christenings of carefree men. The first note of depression is struck at Broken Bow. Clearly some accident occurred here, and there are no more cheerful titles, but only dull surnames such as Gavin, Linscott, and Dunning. The first fine rapture has gone, and I felt no surprise when we came to Dismal River. The spirits of the Old-Timers must have been at their lowest. And rightly is it called Dismal River.

West of that again, the country gets even drearier and drearier. The streams have disappeared and the sand is yellower than ever and the sagebrush drier. By this time a fierce and bitter irony was eating into the souls of the pioneers. Things were so bad that they could conjure up a mocking laugh at their hardships and disillusionments. At least so I read the explanation of Lakeside where there is no lake, and Alliance where nothing meets, and, grimmest joke of all, Nonpareil.

It was a relief to come at last into Wyoming to a wretched little jumble of hovels and shacks, and to get still another proof of the indomitability of the human spirit in its endless war with the cruelty of Nature. For this poor little heap of cabins was labelled, on a huge board, "UPTON, BEST TOWN ON EARTH."

The material assets of the best town on earth were about seventeen rickety huts and about seventeen thousand rusty tins, but its soul was full of unquenchable fire. It was a Don Quixote of a place.

Hour after hour after hour we rolled across the wastes. I read every magazine in the Club-car three times from cover to cover, advertisements and all, not merely the famous story-magazines, *Cosmopolitan*, *Saturday Evening Post*, *Collier's* and so on, but the *Statistical Journal* of the Des Moines Chamber of Commerce, the *Journal* of the Riveters' and Welders' Association of Pittsburgh, Pennsylvania, and the magazine which is devoted to the welfare of the manufacturers of boiler-tubes. There was no alternative, however; the traveller on that train has either to study with the utmost concentration at his command the percentage of aluminium rivets as compared with the percentage of non-ferrous something-or-other in something else, or else to gaze out of the window all day and go mad.

Most of my companions in the Club-car were business-men, and they studied rivets, or whatever it was, unceasingly. They all smoked cigars and did quite a bit of expectoration from time to time. Indeed it was in this train that one of the major insoluble problems of American life obtruded itself upon my attention. Why is it that so many American gentlemen, often of the most distinguished appearance and of otherwise faultless manners, find it necessary to expectorate in public so often, whereas American ladies so very seldom do? In fact, I cannot recall a single instance of seeing an American lady perform this inelegant feat, whereas American gentlemen are at it, in Club-cars at any rate, frequently. I never solved this problem.

I noticed another curious thing in the Club-car. At about midday, a tall, beautifully dressed, handsome, completely *biensoignée* woman came in and sat down in an armchair. She was the first woman of the day to come in, and there were at the time about a dozen men sitting in the car, smoking cigars and poring over their documents. Not one of them paid the slightest attention to her. There were no semi-furtive glances of admiration — and she certainly deserved admiration — no cautious straightening of ties or self-conscious pulling-down of waistcoats. It was just as if she did not exist. She had bright, amused eyes. But these men did not try to catch them. She had a crooked mouth that was full of a gracious frivolity. These men preferred the cuspidor to frivolity. She had a drooping eyelid over one eye that was completely roguish. These men pored over their Import Statistics. At last a diversion occurred. She asked the attendant for an apple. There were no apples on the train, but the man sitting beside her looked up for a moment from his task of cornering something or other and produced an apple out of a small bag. The lady thanked him with a dazzling smile, and a conversation began. After two minutes the man returned to his merger or whatever it was and did not speak another word.

We were in Wyoming by this time and the country grew steadily wilder. The monotony of Nebraskan and Dakotan yellow was being replaced by hot, red soil, and the landscape was covered with thousands of small, red, pyramidal hills like barrows that mark the burial grounds of primaeval warriors, each one divided from its neighbour by steep, stony ravines, dried-up creeks, or shallow rivers. Here and there a miserable, stunted tree stood forlornly by itself.

The small villages, anything from five to twenty miles apart, look almost exactly like the villages of east Poland or the Russian steppes. The houses were always made of wood, except that occasionally there was a square stone building that was obviously a barn or granary, and the faded remnants of blue or green paint upon a shutter or door-lintel were sad reminders of a day when the builder had been proud of his handiwork or the owner proud of his possession. Not once did I see a bright new patch of paint, to show where the spirit of Upton was still fighting against the desert. As in Poland and Russia, the arrival of the train is a great occasion, and the villagers come trooping down to the station to stare at the passengers and exchange a greeting with the engine-drivers. The only real difference between the Wyoming railroad village and the Ukrainian, is that in the former the local church, if it exists, is indistinguishable from the other shacks. In Eastern Europe, the horizon is dotted with sugar-white churches, and green and blue domes.

We passed La Belle Fourche River — that light-hearted, optimistic Frenchman who could see anything belle hereabouts, was a long way from France — and slowly, very slowly, the land became less barren. Stretches of green grass became more frequent; a few cattle appeared; and sometimes there was even a little sparse cultivation. The pioneers must have felt that things were on the upgrade at last, for we came to Felix, and Clear Creek, and Clearmont. There was a feeling of hope in the atmosphere. The colours of the hills were brighter, and the air was clearer, and even the faces of the businessmen in the Club-car assumed an expression of near-intelligence.

And then in front of us, west and north and north-west, spanning the horizon in a mighty curve, burst into view the snowy mountains of Montana, and we were out of the dismal plains at last. Almost at once we were bowling along a pleasant valley, full of cattle and sheep, and dotted with haystacks, and with a stream rolling along between banks that were fringed with real, tall, leafy, flourishing trees, and soon we left Wyoming and entered Montana.

Everything changed quickly, the desolation, the despair, the grimness. The very first halt in Montana was at the hamlet of Wyola — to my disappointment we did not stop at Aberdeen. A special halt there would have been indeed a graceful compliment to a citizen of Aberdeen, Scotland — and on a notice-board, Wyola announced, with infinite jauntiness and a great deal of foresight, that it would be the scene of a Mammoth Rodeo Jamboree on July 4, 1938.

The magnificent blue semicircle of the Big Horn Mountains came nearer and nearer, and as the sun sank behind the snows, we passed the fatal battlefield of the Little Big Horn, where the unfortunate General Custer rode out on June 25, 1876, to fight the Sioux and the Cheyenne and was overwhelmed with all his men by the famous Indians, Sitting Bull and Crazy Horse, Dull Knife and Two Moons and Little Wolf and American Horse and White Bull, and the rest of the plumed and feathered warriors.

I had to change at Billings and wait four hours until nearly midnight for the Northern Pacific express that was to take me on to Helena. I said good-bye without any regret to the Chicago, Burlington and Quincy Railroad. It was not that I objected to the train — it had carried me with safety, comfort, and punctuality — but rather to the country through which it ran. So far as I am concerned, anyone who wants the country between Broken Bow, Nebraska, and Sheridan, Wyoming, can have it. There will be no opposition from me. The old cowpuncher "with his hat throwed back and his spurs a-jingling," spoke a true word when he sang to the little dogies, "It's your misfortune, and none of my own (Whoopee ti yi yo, git along, little dogies), for you know Wyoming will be your new home."

The streets of Billings are well-lit, small hotels and cafés are numerous, and garages abound. I went into the brightest-lit hotel, sat down to dinner, and ordered a Scotch high-ball. I was politely told not only that Montana was a dry state so far as restaurants were concerned, but that the law was observed. This was a serious blow to an old illusion. I had always imagined that the traditions of the lawless Northwest were still alive, that the Sheriff's writ only ran as far as his gun could carry, and that the spirit of the old miner and cow-puncher was untameable even by the most drastic amendments to the Constitution of the United States. Why, in peaceful, semi-Scandinavian, law-abiding Nebraska, no one paid any attention to the drink-laws. Surely in wild, son-of-a-gun Montana, they would hardly have heard of Prohibition, let alone continued to be Dry after Repeal. But it was only too true. There is no need for Vigilantes of the Pussyfoot movement to organize themselves for the suppression of the lawless drinkers. The lawless drinkers are too law-abiding for that, and the great James Williams of whom the monument records that he was the "Captain of the Vigilantes through whose untiring efforts and intrepid daring Law and Order were established in Montana," seems to have done his work too thoroughly.

But I could not help wondering what James Williams would have thought of it all. He was quick with his gun, and resolute in the stamping out of crime, but I could find no record that he was a teetotaller or was interested in preventing his friends from drinking a high-ball when they felt so inclined.

There was only one place in all Billings where I could legally buy a bottle of Scotch whisky, and that was in the State liquor-store. Temporarily abandoning my dinner, therefore, I ran through the night to the State liquor-store, put down my five dollars and asked for a bottle of Johnny Walker.

"Have you got your State licence to buy liquor?" asked the store-keeper.

I recoiled in horror. The spirit of the lawless cow-puncher had sunk even lower than I had feared.

"No," I said. "Is it necessary?"

"It is, son," replied the man.

"Where can I get a permit?"

"At the Municipal Building [or it may have been County, or City, or Police, Building — I cannot remember] to-morrow between the hours of ten and four,"

"But I want a drink now," I protested.

"Isn't that just too bad?" was the unsympathetic answer.

"Well," I said, stung into an unwonted vehemence by his lack of sympathy, "I've come six thousand miles from Scotland to see your blank, blank, super-blank State of Montana, and it's a bit hard that I can't buy a bottle of my own native drink without one of your blank, blank, super-blank permits."

The entire staff of the liquor-store was galvanized into activity in a flash.

"Are you from Scotland?" exclaimed the store keeper. "Why the hell didn't you say so before? Of course you can have whisky and as much as you like. To hell with the State permit!"

After a lot of hand-shaking and expressions of mutual esteem, I departed, bottle snug in pocket, back to my dinner.

But progress back was not so easy. The sidewalks were suddenly crowded with people, and an occasional cop was asking folks not to use the streets. The reason was soon obvious. It was now late October and the electoral fever which I had noticed in the exhortations and appeals on the road out of Omaha, was steadily mounting, and a torch-light procession was coming past. The politicians of Billings, whatever their short comings, defects, and general inability to conjure Utopia out of a hat may be, have grasped one universal, fundamental principle of human nature that has apparently been concealed to their Omahan confrères. They have hit upon the eternal Truth that it is more difficult to attract a crowd by exhibiting photographs of stoutish, pasty-faced, horn-rimmed candidates for the popular fancy, than by parading a bevy of pretty girls in velveteen trousers. The torch-light procession was almost entirely made up of pretty girls in velveteen trousers, and the crowds of admirers and sympathizers on the sidewalks was, in consequence, very large. Indeed, the onlookers found it almost impossible to tear themselves away until the last of the ravishing torch-bearers had disappeared. When the last of the torch-bearers had disappeared, I returned to my belated dinner which tasted all the better for the draughts of my national drink with which it was accompanied. I paid for my dinner with a ten-dollar note and was staggered to get my change in great, shining, silver, cart-wheel dollars. They were the first that I had seen.

As I strolled back to the station — which, by the way, had now become a Deepo — I could not ascertain the exact whereabouts of the Mason and Dixon Line which separates the Stations from the Deepos — I passed a shop-window which seemed to me to be one of the saddest things I had ever seen. It was empty of goods, it was grimy with long disuse, its glass was cracked. There was no name across the top, and a few advertisements hung, tattered and soiled, from the door-post, and the paint was cracked on the door. Across the window-pane ran, in big, defiant letters, the slogan, "We buy and sell most anything,"

The Northern Pacific express thundered in to the Deepo and I commended my soul once again to Botolph, patron saint of wayfarers, and my person once again to an African.

CHAPTER NINE

We primeval forests felling,
We the rivers stemming, vexing we and piercing deep the
    mines within,
We the surface broad surveying, we the virgin soil upheaving,
    Pioneers! O Pioneers!

WALT WHITMAN

Helena, Montana, is rightly named after a figure of Romance, for Helena itself is a Romantic town. It lies on the slopes of the Montana Rockies, about forty-five hundred feet above sea-level, and on the west are the higher mountains, on the east a broad valley. Nothing more romantic about that, you say, than about any page in any Baedeker. Just wait a minute. It was in 1864 that gold was discovered where Helena is now, twelve years before Crazy Horse and Sitting Bull destroyed Custer three hundred miles and more to the east, between the gold-discoverers and the Mississippi River. The discoverers must have come up from the Southwest, for they brought with them the phrase "placer-mining," which is simply a corruption of the Spanish word *plaza*, or place where minerals are found. So it must have been from the Spanish Southwest, from California and Nevada and Arizona, that the first prospectors came across the Rockies into Montana. They were bold men and they cared as little for Crazy Horse as for grizzly bears. They struck gold in a narrow winding creek which they called Last Chance Gulch, and the Gulch is the Main Street of Helena today. My encyclopaedia — a smart, up-to-date, expensive one — tells me that in Helena, "many of the streets are wide and straight, shaded with rows of cottonwood trees, and faced with handsome residences and business premises." So they are. My encyclopaedia has not lied to me. But I care not a straw for Helena's wide and straight streets. All the essence of the Romance of the Northwest is in that narrow curly street which runs steadily uphill where the gold used to lie. Thirty million dollars of gold were taken out of Last Chance Gulch by placer-mining, and when, not so long ago, a new hotel was built on Main Street, eight hundred dollars of gold dust came out of the foundation-hole. Thank Heaven that the citizens of Helena have a sense of the fitness of things, and when the proprietors of the hotel came to give it a name, they did not call it, as we would have called it in Europe, the Ritz or the Carlton or even the Ritz-Carlton or the Majestic or the Splendid or any other meaningless international jargon of sounds. They called it simply the Placer Hotel in memory of the placer-miners who made Last Chance Gulch into the flourishing city of Helena, capital of a State that is five times the size of Scotland.

Walk up that narrow little street, between its simple rows of unpretentious shops, and you come suddenly out of Main Street into the old Gulch. Civilization drops away behind you, and you are back in the strong old days of the sixties when all the world, so far as the placer-miners knew, was young. Stone and mortar and neat commercial architecture come to an end, and in the tiny valley, overhung with pine-clad hillsides, you stumble on log-cabins of the early days. They are squat and square, and the logs are unshaped, and the crevices between the roundnesses of the logs are filled with white plaster. The old Posting House still stands beside the road, and near it there is another building, believed to have been at one time also a Posting House, which is unique in my experience of architecture. It is more than likely that it is unique in the world, and certainly Montana ought to cherish it as an "ancient monument" of very great importance. The ground floor is an ordinary Old-Timer's cabin — strong and primitive. But the amazing thing about it is that there is a second storey, built in the true tradition of Elizabethan England. Lovely reddish pink bricks and cross beams (made of cedar instead of oak) in the old pattern of uprights, laterals, and curving supports, the second storey might have come straight from a Buckinghamshire village of the Tudor times. What in the name of Heaven it is doing in the bottom of Last Chance Gulch, six thousand miles from Tudor Buckinghamshire, and who in the name of Heaven built it, and whatever made the builder think of putting it on top of an Old-Timer's log-cabin, are dark mysteries.

Turn up the hill, for a moment, to the right of the Gulch and you are plunged still deeper into the Romance of the pioneering days. Reeder Street is perhaps a hundred yards long, uphill into the side of the Gulch, and there are perhaps twenty or thirty little houses on it, and in it you will see ancient men sitting in the sun at their doors plying ancient trades, working away with bits of metal or bits of wood, sharpening hand-tools, cutting, filing, hammering, and so intent, each upon his small task, that they do not peer up at the passing stranger.

The earliest house of all is the Gilpatrick house, within a yard of Reeder Street. And if there is Romance in the Gulch and the old cabins and the ancient craftsmen, there is double Romance in the Gilpatrick house. For not only is it the earliest of them, but in front of it grow two tall locust-trees which were brought as seedlings in tomato-cans by the Gilpatricks on their long journey from the East in their covered wagon.

As it climbs higher into the hills, Last Chance Gulch turns into Grizzly Gulch. The whole scene is very like Scotland, a stream rippling down among willow-saplings, pine-trees and mountains. Only the stones are yellower than in Scotland.

The road twists and turns up Grizzly Gulch, and the heaps of soil and grass-covered stones beside the bed of the stream mark the labours of the pioneer placer-miners, and of their successors, the thrifty Chinamen who worked over the soil for gold-dust which had escaped the careless, free-and-easy methods of the pioneers. I walked up the road, musing upon such hackneyed themes as "Departed Glory", "Desolation where used to be Human Activity", and "Dead Industries", and misquoting to myself such extracts from Omar Khayyám as I could recall that might be appropriate. Ichabod, I fancy, was frequently on my lips as I strolled along. Needless to say, I was completely wrong and all my philosophical reflections were wasted.

For I came upon two men who were very busy in the bed of the sapling-filled creek below the road and I fell into conversation with them. They were big strong men, brothers, with slow smiles and slow speech. I asked them casually what they were doing and, to my discomfiture and ill-concealed chagrin, they replied politely that they were placer-mining.

"Placer-mining!" I cried. "But I thought placer-mining was dead and buried these thirty years."

"Maybe so," they answered, "but it's come to life again." And they told me the whole story, how placer-mining is unprofitable with gold at twenty dollars an ounce, but at thirty-five an ounce it becomes profitable again, how even the Chinamen had left some behind, how it was better to work for three dollars a week than to hang about the streets of Helena and draw Relief, and how the mountains were full of men doing the same.

All my moralizing fell to the ground at one blow. So far from being a dead industry in a dead country, gold-mining was a thriving and growing industry, and the Pioneers were abroad in the hills once again. The men of '64 in Montana did not look to the State or the Federal Government to support them, and the men of to-day seemed to feel the same way about things.

I sat down on a tree-trunk and was given a demonstration in the art of panning gold, and then, having mastered the principles, I took a pan myself and set to work while the two brothers, having overcome their disappointment at finding that I was not Mr. Ramsay MacDonald, returned to their labours.

(Incidentally, their labours consisted of digging a tunnel slap under the main motor-road. I asked them if nobody objected to having tunnels dug slap under the main motor-roads of Montana, and they scratched their heads and said that they had not thought about it, but it was a free country anyway.)

After half an hour's hard work with my pan, I began to think that perhaps there was more in panning than I had thought; but after three-quarters of an hour I was able to display, with a good deal of pride, a prodigious quantity of gold-dust among the gravel. The brothers emerged from their tunnel and shook their heads sadly.

"Fool's gold, fool's gold," they murmured.

"What the devil do you mean by fool's gold?" I shouted indignantly. My arms were aching intolerably and my back was cracking.

"Mica," they said, and retired into the tunnel.

After an hour and twenty minutes I had finished the pan, and the result was four grains of real gold dust, gleaming bravely if somewhat forlornly in their conspicuous isolation upon the black sand.

"You'll never make money that way," I said.

The brothers gazed solemnly at my pan. "We would have done it quicker," said one of them, "and only got three grains. But a Scotchman couldn't bear losing a grain. That's why you were so slow." And they guffawed with delight.

I strolled back through the woods. The ground was red with the berries of the kinnikinnick, and from somewhere high above me on the hillside came the click of metal upon stone where some other Pioneer was at work.

That evening I came upon one of the most remarkable newspaper paragraphs which it has ever been my good fortune to see. It occurred in the Helena *Daily Independent*, and ran as follows:

VITAL STATISTICS

DEATHS

Mrs. Amelia Milch, 67, of 534 South Rodney Street.
Martin A. Terwilliger, 38, of Stratton, Neb.

Sousa's band was heard only once by his mother; it made her so nervous that she never went to hear it again.

And, as if this was not enough joy for one evening, after dinner that night I was taken by friends, to whom I am in consequence indebted for ever, to a Wrestling Tournament.

There were about five hundred of us packed into the Masonic Hall that is called the Shrine on Masonic occasions, and the Shrine Arena when a bout of wrestling is toward, and we wore anything from gent's lounge suitings to blue shirts, shaggy trousers and ten-gallon hats. The walls were covered with national flags, and the selection was a very queer one. There were two gigantic Stars and Stripes, one upside-down, two Turkish flags and one each of Sweden, Norway, and Spain. Then came, most mysteriously and at the same time to me most gratifyingly, the Royal Standard of Scotland, and next to it Siam and then the British Red Ensign.

But there was no time to ask questions about the flags, for Referee Foster, in grey trousers and white sweater, was clambering nimbly into the ring, and the miners and cowboys were giving a great "hand" to the Ref.

Mr. Foster was a remarkable figure. He always refereed these contests, apparently, because he was so indisputably the best wrestler, boxer, and all-in fighter, in Montana, that nobody could be persuaded to go into the ring against him, and that is saying a lot in a crowd of pretty tough North-western miners and ranchers. There was nothing left for him, therefore, but to referee.

When the applause had subsided, the Ref. announced the first match. "Bob Macaulay [wild cheering] at 163 pounds against Sammy Morgan [tornado of booing and hissing] at 161 pounds, eight rounds of ten minutes each, two out of three falls to win,"

Mr. Macaulay, an honest-looking, rather muddle-headed fellow, slouched forward and bowed to his enthusiastic supporters, and then Mr. Morgan walked forward and sneered at the audience. The more they yelled at him, the more open became his derision, and when a particularly violent tornado of cat-calls shivered the rafters of the Shrine, he made an expressive gesture of contempt with his thumb, forefingers and nose, and a row of cowboys in blue shirts just behind us began to shuffle their feet and one or two half-rose from their seats as if meditating a rush at the ring.

When the match started, it was soon obvious why Mr. Morgan was not the darling of the crowd. The moment Bob began to get a firm grip on some part of his anatomy, Sammy made a galvanic wriggle, dived through the ropes, scuttled round outside the ring and jumped in at the other side, and fell upon the slow-witted Bob in the rear while that worthy was still wondering where his opponent had got to. Sammy spent at least half the time racing round outside the ring, and the audience got madder than ever, and poor Bob got almost giddy trying to spin round fast enough in the middle of the ring to keep his adversary in view. Once or twice Sammy came a little too close and Bob enveloped him in a bear-like hug, but each time Sammy just managed to reach the ropes in time, and as soon as he got half over the edge of the platform, the Force of Gravity did the rest and both wrestlers went out together. Simple Bob, a man of one idea, was strongly in favour on these occasions of continuing the match among the ringside-seats, but he soon found that Ref. Foster had other ideas, and he sadly let go of Sammy's neck, ear, left ankle, right shoulder-blade, and waist, and climbed sulkily back into the ring, while Sammy nipped round to the other side, blew a kiss to the raging crowd, and prepared to resume hostilities. But by this time poor Bob was so obsessed with the injustice of the world, and so bewildered by the eel-like tactics of his adversary, that he advanced with a sort of half-hearted carelessness, and, to the horror of the cowboys and miners, was overwhelmed in a trice by the nimble Sam and flung heavily to the ground. First fall to Mr. Morgan.

Pandemonium raged in the Shrine. Even the flag of Siam seemed to ripple sympathetically, and it appeared to me that once or twice Mr. Morgan glanced anxiously towards the door marked "Exit," and that he was not quite so free with his smile of derision as before.

The second round opened ominously. Sammy, penned in a corner, made his usual dive out of the ring and a piece of sausage whizzed past his ear as he got up, followed by a meat-pie of some kind and the rung of a chair. A moment later Ref. Foster announced that Sam Morgan abandoned the match, having injured his collar-bone in falling out of the ring, and that the next contest would be between Lumberman Pound and Louie Floyd.

It soon transpired that handsome, curly-headed young Louie was the idol of the crowd, and that the Lumberman was universally held to be the dirtiest fighter in Montana. As the match went on, I did not know whether to be sorrier for the unfortunate Louie or for the brutal Lumberman. Every time the Lumberman got a foot or hand free he either kicked Louie or illegally punched him, and each time Ref. Foster kicked or punched the Lumberman. On one rare occasion Louie got a rather awkward half-Nelson, or some thing, on the Lumberman and the latter only extricated himself by getting hold of the pretty curls and giving them a violent tug. Whereupon the Ref. seized the Lumberman's black mop with both hands and dragged him round the ring. This was more than the fine old blood of the Pounds could stand, and he leapt to his feet and made a rush at Mr. Foster. But the Ref. knew the game by heart and he dropped on one knee in a most sinister way and awaited the assault. It was just like a terrier and an experienced cat. The Lumberman's heart failed him, he hesitated, stopped, and was trying to make up his mind what to do, when he was seized from behind by the resourceful Mr. Floyd and dashed to the boards.

One down and two to play, Mr. Pound's tactics became even dirtier than before, and the Ref. was kept busy punching, wrestling, and hair-tugging. At last the climax came. Poor Louie, who was playing a very third fiddle, fell on his head and was instantly kicked on the ear by the Lumberman, who was promptly uppercut by Mr. Foster. The Lumberman, in desperation, let loose a wild swing at the Ref. and missed that agile gentleman by yards, and then, realizing the fatal rashness of the act, he sprang over the ropes and bolted for the door, Ref. Foster also sprang over the ropes and bolted after him. But terror added yards on to the Lumberman's normal sprinting form and he maintained his lead. Just as he vanished, Mr. Foster picked up a chair with great dexterity and slung it after him. The chair missed, however, and went through a plate-glass window, with a crash that restored everyone's good humour.

Then came the cream of the evening's entertainment, the Rassle Royal. Five wrestlers in the Ring simultaneously, all against all, no time limit, and the survivor wins. We all lay back in our seats and a sort of sigh of content ran round the Hall.

The five heroes were: Finky Nelson, a mild and inoffensive youth, short of stature and with square shoulders; Mike Muldooney; John (Whiskers) Moses, a large man in a green vest and adorned with an enormous black beard. Mr. Moses was the champion and idol of the local House of David; the Black Jaguar was the fourth, a lissom, elegant negro with a coppery skin that looked as if it had been polished with Simoniz, sleek hair, and a dazzling smile; and lastly, a tall, superciliously self-confident man, with long sinewy arms, the redoubtable, hated, feared, Totem-Pole Johnson.

Ref. Foster sprang into the Ring and the Rassle Royal was on. It was the wildest chaos. There were no allies, no prearranged partnerships. I had imagined that the other four would make a dead-set at the terrible Totem-Pole and eliminate him at once, but nothing of the sort happened. At first Mike seemed to be getting the short end of the straw, with three of them kneeling on him, but the Jaguar created a diversion by yielding to his fatal sense of humour. Mr. Moses's massive posterior was irresistibly extended towards him and the Jaguar, with a vast grin, kicked it sharply and fled, hotly pursued by the Ref. and the injured party. Then Finky seemed to be in trouble but was saved by a sudden attempt by the Totem-Pole and the Son of David to eliminate the Jaguar, who only escaped by dodging out of the ring. When he came back, the other four were jumbled in one mass of arms and legs on the floor, so the Jaguar contributed his little bit of fun by taking a running high-jump and landing on the top of the heap. But the pace was too hot to last, and the black-bearded champion of the House of David was the first to go, with a broken arm. Then Muldooney made his fatal mistake. In side-stepping the Totem-Pole, he came down heavily on the Ref.'s toe. With a hoarse cry of pain, the Ref. tripped him up, and the other three fell on him with a whoop, and he was out. Then Finky and the Totem-Pole, feeling perhaps that blood will tell, combined against the Jaguar who, after racing twenty or thirty times round outside the ring, was persuaded to return and was duly annihilated.

That left only poor little Finky and the Totem-Pole, with his superior smile and his octopus arms, to wrestle two falls out of three. Amid explosions of wrath and thunders of cat-calls, the Totem-Pole soon demolished Finky and won the first fall. But in the second bout he made, probably through over-confidence, a fatal slip, and in a trice Finky had him in the deadliest of all locks. He had got hold of the Totem-Pole's ankles and was whirling him round and round as if he was Nijinsky and Mr. Johnson was Karsavina. Higher and higher he swung the unfortunate Totem and then dashed the back of his head on the boards as if he was using a hammer to drive in a nail.

In the third round the Totem-Pole was completely dazed, and in a jiffy Finky had him by the ankles again, whirled him round again, and dashed his head on the boards again, and the Rassle Royal was over. Little Finky Nelson had won.

The news soon spread round Helena and its environs that I had so conspicuously mastered the art of placer-mining that I had actually panned four grains in an hour and twenty minutes, and it was generally felt in North-western metallurgical circles that I might as well devote an hour or two to acquiring a similar mastery over the allied technique of quartz-mining and large-scale dredging, and, if time permitted, over the indispensable business of smelting.

Accordingly, my hospitable host and hostess arranged for an excursion to the mining-town of Marysville, situated in the mountains above Helena.

We started off towards the west, and motored along Prickly Pear Valley (which is sometimes called Scratch Gravel Valley), a dry plain covered with sage-grass, until we came to the real mountains. The valley-walls close in on each side, and grew steeper and rockier. Below the road was the dried-up bed of a river full of crimson-stemmed willows that made a fine show of colour against the drab pines and grey stones, and suddenly we turned a corner and there, at the junction of five valleys, was the Ghost City, the mining-camp of Marysville.

It was some time about 1878 that the illiterate Irishman, Tommy Cruse, came over the hills from Silver Creek where he had been placer-mining, and found the famous mine which he christened the Drum Lummon. Old Tommy Cruse could neither read nor write, but he knew the value of a mine when he saw it, and he ultimately sold the Drum Lummon to an English company for $1,500,000 and, because he distrusted cheques, he insisted on being paid at least half a million in gold dollars. It was the finding of this great mine that made Marysville, and a town, built of stone and slate, sprang up around the dotted log-and-plaster cabins, and the railroads came up the valley from Helena.

But it did not last, and the town dwindled and dwindled. The younger, more adventurous spirits packed their tools and set out to find new prospects, the older ones stayed on and died one by one, until only the shell of a town was left, and the slates began to fall from the roof of the Baptist chapel, and skunks and rabbits scuttled in and out of the derelict saloons, and birds made their nests in the store, and the paint flaked off the door of the Masonic Hall.

It was a strange sensation, wandering on the grassy streets of this dead town. Names are still faintly legible on some of the shops; here there is an advertisement for caps, eight dollars each; there is a notice on a saloon of some passing troupe of entertainers; faded lettering and figures announce that the Masonic Hall was built in 1884; the tiny churches, Episcopalian, Presbyterian, and Baptist, are decaying, and the school is empty, and one small wooden hut is labelled "Barber: Baths."

I spoke to an old lady who had lived in Marysville for forty-eight years, and had not left it even in its days of desolation. She was a beautiful old lady, with clear, blue eyes and a comely old face and the manners of a duchess. Her name was Mrs. Larsen.

"I saw Marysville when it was nothing," said Mrs. Larsen, "and I saw it grow to three thousand people, and I saw it go down to nothing again, and now I see it coming up again. The people are coming back and the mines are working. I saw the first school-teacher come up the valley and begin school for the children, and I remember the time when there were eight teachers and a Superintendent, and then the time came when there weren't any teachers at all, just like it was when I was a girl. I remember when they brought the railroad up the valley, and I remember, when everything was dead, how they came and took the railroad away again."

I asked if Marysville had been a very wild place in the height of its prosperity, and was rather surprised when Mrs. Larsen shook her head.

"Marysville was never a wild place," she said. "There were six or eight saloons besides hotels and cafés, but it was not wild. Not to be compared with Helena. I had an uncle who came from the East to Helena many, many years ago and the first thing he saw was a man hanging on a tree at the edge of the town. My uncle turned round and went back to the East and never crossed the Mississippi for the rest of his life.

"The mines are working again now," repeated Mrs. Larsen, "but things will never be the same again now that the Englishmen have gone. They were splendid employers. I wish the English were back again."

I asked her if she knew who the Mary was after whom the town had been called. "It was Mary Ralston," she said at once. "Pretty Mary Ralston. She and Ralston were among the first to come up the valley. He worked with Tommy Cruse after he had found the Drum Lummon, and when the people came and built houses and the town had to get a name, Tommy called it after Mary. She's dead many a year ago."

The air seemed to be full of ghosts as the old woman rambled on about long-forgotten miners, and the great days of the Pioneers. I saw two more ghosts before I left the Ghost City. One was the stamping-mill that crushes the Drum Lummon quartz. We knocked on various doors and, getting no answer, finally pushed one open and went in. It was like a design by Piranesi attempting to make a caricature of himself. It was dark, and ramshackle, and rickety. It was like a toy that has been built by one generation of boys, and then added to and added to by successive generations, haphazardly and at random. Nothing seemed to fit anything else. There was a perfect labyrinth of beams, bars, trap-doors, insecure platforms, wobbly plank-bridges, shoots, crushers, tubs, cauldrons, wheels, ropes, and pulleys. Everything was made of wood. We wandered round, tripping, stumbling, bumping our heads, and poising ourselves over perilous abysses, and nobody paid the slightest attention to us. Indeed there was no one in the mill to pay attention to us. There was no movement, either human or mechanical, save in one corner where a machine was churning up a cauldron of water. It was a ghost of a mill.

The other ghost which I saw before I left Marysville was the blackened ruin of "the Englishman's house." The mine-managers of the Drum Lummon had lived there in the days of the English company, and the house was accidentally burnt down a few years ago. Three things they left behind them, three things that are so much part of the English heritage and the English tradition that they can be found all over the world wherever the English go. A stable for their horses, a formal garden for their flowers, and an open fireplace.

The stable at the Drum Lummon is derelict, and the flowers have overrun the edges of their beds and have mingled sadly with the weeds, but in all the ruin of the house itself, where no brick rests upon any other brick, the open fireplace stands up proudly and undefeated, as much a part of the Mother-country as Windsor Castle or the Tower of London.

I finished off my metallurgical education before turning aside to master the intricacies of Montana's other great trade — sheep and cattle — and visited a large dredge that was working in a river away below the town, and the local smelting works. The dredge was placer-mining on a huge, mechanized scale. The river had been gone over and over by pioneers and Chinamen, but the dredge worked so fast and scooped out such masses of gravel at each dive into the muddy water, that it could make a profit at five cents of gold per ton. But this noisy, prosaic, dull machine takes all the Romance out of mining and reduces an individual art to clumsy mass-production, and after a few minutes I left it to its prosaic task.

My visit to the smelting-works was interesting for two reasons. One reason was that it was the first smelter I had seen in America. Later on, I discovered that it is the ambition of every American man but not, I am thankful to say, of every American woman to take visitors over the local smelting-works. It is almost an obsession. Over and over again I have taken part in the following dialogue, and on each occasion the words of the dialogue have been practically identical.

KIND HOST: Now what would you like to do to-day?

MYSELF: I should like to walk around and have a look at your city.

KIND HOST: Fine! I've got the automobile at the door and we'll drive out to see the smelting-works. Would you like to see the smelting-works?

MYSELF (*as tactfully as possible*): I'd sooner walk in the town.

KIND HOST: Fine! Well go out to the smelter at once.

MYSELF: I think I'd sooner not. I've seen lots of smelters already.

KIND HOST: Oh, but you must see *our* smelter. You'll like *our* smelter.

MYSELF (*almost in tears*): I don't want to see any smelter.

KIND HOST: It's no trouble at all. It's a pleasure for me. Jump right in, and we'll go and see the smelter. (*I jump right in and we go off to see the smelter.*)

As I say, this was the invariable procedure, and I must have visited dozens of smelters during my travels in the western States of the Union. At least it certainly seemed to be dozens, and I fancy that I am probably the finest amateur smelter alive to-day.

But it was different at Helena. I had not yet been through the mill, so to speak. And the second reason why I was interested at Helena was the personality of the manager. Although American-born of American-born parents, he was a Scot of Scots. He was a young man, in the middle thirties, and he looked like a Highlander, and he thought like a Highlander, and he bore a fine old Highland name. By the Grace of Heaven, his clan was one that had been for some centuries in friendly alliance with mine (they became friendly after a stormy beginning), and so we were able to talk to each other. Had he been a Campbell, or even a MacGregor, I might be one smelter short

100

in my experience. But fortunately for both of us, he was not, and I was able to go round the works and listen to his crystal-clear explanations of highly technical processes and watch the sequence of events by which a heap of dull-looking soil is transmuted into a shining, splashing, silvery torrent of molten lead.

Having thus acquired a sound knowledge of the science of Metallurgy, I turned back to the wide-open spaces and went off to see the sheep-country.

It was a long drive up into the mountains. We passed Silver City, a proud municipality that contains three houses, Canyon Creek City which has two houses less than Silver City, and Georgeville. Georgeville has no houses at all, but there are four logs lying by the roadside where Georgeville used to be. On each side of the road there were innumerable traces of mining, washing, and prospecting, some of them old and moss- grown, many of them obviously brand-new.

The road went up and up through the canyons. A few cottonwood trees still wore their last, lingering, golden leaves, but the fir-trees darkened the scene with their sombre foliage, and even the masses of red willows and the green-yellow glittering trunks of the leafless aspens could not relieve the shadowy gloom of these narrow defiles through the rocks. Once or twice we climbed a canyon whose precipitous walls were streaked with red and purple streaks where the ice had passed slowly by, but in the main the colouring was drab. It was like Browning's "great wild country" where

> ... at a funeral pace
> Round about, solemn and slow,
> One by one, row after row,
> Up and up the pine-trees go,
> So, like black priests up, and so
> Down the other side again ...

And then the automobile climbed a last slope in the long ascent and ran out on to a level patch of road and stopped. We were at the Continental Divide, six thousand feet up. The air was clear and fresh and full of the scent of the pines, and very silent. Below us lay the Pacific side, and the valley far down was greener and lighter than on the Atlantic side, and the grass was riper and the trees were gayer. In the distance storm-clouds were gathering, and high above them, high into the blueness, soared the full cold splendour of the Rocky Mountains.

We dropped down the Pacific slope of the Divide and came to a sheep-farm among the woods. There was a bustle of activity round the log-cabins, and horses were being saddled, and packs were being loaded, for the weekly pack-train was about to start on its round of the lonely sheep-herders on the hillsides. These men, mostly Romanians, live all by themselves for month after month and year after year, until they have acquired such a habit of solitude that they will often walk away if a stranger seems likely to open a conversation with them, and on the rare occasions when they find themselves in company will sit in impenetrable silence for hours. Once in every two or three years they will draw all their savings (and they have been earning fifty dollars a month and all found, with no opportunity of spending) and go into the nearest town, and within a week they will have been robbed of every cent, usually by brother-Romanians, and then they will go back to another two or three years of solitude on their sheep-range.

As my hostess appeared to be anxious to take a photograph of a Scottish traveller in a place where few Scottish travellers had penetrated for some years, the men who were harnessing the pack-train suggested eagerly that I should pose for the camera seated on the back of the leading horse of the pack-train. Unwilling to disgrace my country by seeming to be reluctant for any adventure, I put as good a face upon it as I could, and prepared to mount. But there was something so eager, so expectant, so all-on-tiptoe, about the attitude of the sheepmen, that I paused for a moment. They were like children waiting for the curtain to rise at their pantomime. Foot in the stirrup, I asked them what was up. They looked confused and embarrassed, more like children than ever, and finally one of them explained that the last time anyone had mounted that particular horse, it had bolted into the woods, and the rider had lost all the skin off his face, and they were curious to know if it would happen again. In all the age-long history of horsemanship, I do not suppose that any foot has ever come out of any stirrup more quickly than mine did, and the subsequent photograph was taken of a Scottish gentleman standing firmly upon the ground, grasping the horse's bridle, and in full possession of all the skin on his face. The sheepmen were bitterly disappointed.

We left the sheep-farm in the woods — and I shall never forget the mixture of scents in that warm, windless valley, the pungent, acrid smell of the sheep, the scent of the pines, and the drifting smoke from the wood-fire in the log-cabin and motored on to the ranch itself, and there an ambition of more than thirty years standing was realized. I met a real, old-time, pioneering cowboy. He was a small, thin, brown man, very wiry, very silent, and almost ninety years old. In 1870 Mr. S. came first to Montana and those were tough days in the North-west. It was only six years after the Vigilantes had cleaned up the road-agents and hanged the iniquitous Sheriff Henry Plummer and his gang of desperadoes at Bannack City, and eight years before Chief Joseph led the Nez Perce Indians to battle on the banks of the Clearwater River. In the old days of the "national domains," Mr. S. had wandered with his cattle from pasturage to pasturage for thirty-five years. "I just pirated around," said Mr. S. And then, when the days of wandering were over and the settlers began to acquire the domains and the era of private ownership began, Mr. S. bought land and became a ranch-owner.

I asked him about the Indians, hoping against hope for tales of desperate encounters, of hideous torture heroically endured, of tremendous rides across the mountains to warn outlying farms that the Chiefs were on the War Path, of stubborn defences of stockades, of grim discoveries of the scalped bodies of old pals. But Mr. S. was sadly prosaic about it all. "I did a big ride once," he admitted, "when Chief Joseph was out in these parts, to warn my brother, and I found him sound asleep in his camp as if there wasn't an Indian in Montana. But there never was much danger from Indians. Sometimes in the night a creeper would try to get up close, but in the daytime we just used to signal to them to keep away."

"And they kept away?" I asked sadly.

"Oh, yes," replied Mr. S.

"Simply because of a signal?" I asked in despair.

"Oh, yes," replied Mr. S. "You see, most of them were cowards."

I changed the subject. "Montana must be very different to what it used to be," I said, and Mr. S. agreed.

"In the days when Chief Joseph was out," said Mr. S., "I used to ride everywhere. Then the roads came, and I was able to take the wagon up to the ranch. After that the railroad came to Helena, and then we all bought automobiles. But now I find it best to fly up to the ranch."

Mr. S. was eighty-two when he flew for the first time, but now there is a regular landing-ground at the ranch. The Spirit of the Pioneers dies hard.

Looking at this broad, peaceful, grassy valley in the mountains, with its flocks of grazing sheep, its snug buildings, its garage, its flying-ground, its roads, I found it extraordinarily difficult to realize that its whole history is covered by the span of a single life. Mr. S. was nearly twenty years of age when the first owner of the ranch was murdered by the Indians with all his children and his Indian wife (an iron railing encloses the grave, and the man who lugged an iron railing all those miles up into the mountains was one of great piety or great craziness), and there was Mr. S. skipping nimbly over ditches, flying round the country in aeroplanes, and trying to bamboozle vagrant Scotsmen into "sitting in to a little poker-game." With native caution I declined to be blandished into his little poker-game, and I was told afterwards that I was extremely wise. For Mr. S. was a demon at the game.

On our way back into Helena, between interminable fields of short grass and sagebrush, smelling strongly after a shower of rain, and the comical tumbleweed that goes bowling along in the wind like diminutive haystacks that are playing hookey, we came round a bend in the road, and there below us were the waters of the Missouri,, shining very blue in the sun between the dark cliffs of the defile which Lewis and Clark called the Gates of the Mountains when they came up on their immortal journey. Nearby I found an election appeal which beat any that I had yet discovered. Mr. Frank H., running for District Judge on an Independent ticket, pledged himself to secure "better conditions for Labour, Farmers, and hard pressed Debtors, without regard to refined technicalities." If ever a man deserved election it was Frank. He would have had my vote every time. Would that there were more like him, both in the United States and in Great Britain.

There is a mining-camp in Montana which embodies in its name a very strange piece of literary appreciation and judgment. In a deep, narrow, sunless canyon in the mountains lies an old wooden village, once prosperous like Marysville, then a ghost, and now reviving again. At first it was called Red Mountain. Then, presumably, a miner named Russell struck a rich vein and his influence became powerful, for the name was changed to Russellville. Incidentally it is curious that he should have been so much more successful at giving a name to a camp than to his children. He found no difficulty about Russellville, but he was sorely bothered about his family. For he was very anxious to launch them into the world with a proper quota of two names apiece, but his small supply ran out and he was compelled to christen one of them "L. George Russell," the L. not standing for anything at all. The Russell star must have waned. Perhaps his mining operations petered out, perhaps he grew so rich that he left the district. Anyway, Russellville became Clarkston for a while. Then the influence of Clark declined before an inrush of new settlers, and Clarkston became Young Ireland. Now comes the strange episode in which the Poetical Drama suddenly hurtled into the rough lives of this tiny community. One day, many years ago, the news arrived at this lonely canyon that a touring company of actors was billed for a theatrical performance in Helena. Such visits must have been rare in the old days, and the miners of Young Ireland determined to make a gala occasion out of this one. They put on their smartest clothes, saddled their horses, and rode off to Helena. Next day they came galloping back in a roaring, exalted, frantic state of enthusiasm. The play which they had seen had been an unforgettable moment in their lives, and Young Ireland was to be Young Ireland no longer.

The miners, their heads aflame with Romance and Poesy, rechristened their mining-camp Rimini, for the playwright of the piece was Stephen Phillips and the play was *Paolo and Francesca*. And so to this day the little mining-camp is called, with the accent heavily on the last syllable, after the ancient city of the Malatesti.

Just as I had the luck to meet, In Mr. S., an Old-Timer of the cattle-ranges, so in Rimini I met an Old-Timer of the mining-camps. In a tiny, one-roomed, wooden shack, warmed by a stove and lit by an old oil- lamp, decorated with calendars of decades ago and advertisements of long-forgotten wares, sat old Jack Kelly, cooking his evening meal. Eighty-five years of age, his face and neck were seamed and lined and criss-crossed with wrinkles, and browned by the winds and storms to the colour of stained oak. His hands were thin and hard and almost black, and the skin was drawn so tightly across the knuckles that it shone in the lamplight and his bristly head of close-cut iron-grey hair was without a trace of baldness. He wore corduroy trousers that looked as if they were made of the same material as his face and neck, and a purple coat with ragged fringes. I do not think I ever saw a man who was so thin and frail. His bones were pushing out against his skin.

But old Jack Kelly has no complaints against his poverty or his thinness. Every morning of his life he gets up and cooks his own breakfast, saddles his horse and rides up the Red Mountain to his Prospect, works there all day and rides home in the evening to his hut, carrying his day's ore for the smelter.

I asked him if he had always been a miner. "Always," he said, "ever since I went into the lead-mines in Wisconsin when I was seven years old. My father was a lead-miner and he brought us up on mining. Seventy-eight years I've been at it." A ghost of an ancient smile flickered on his thin cracked lips and a glint of light shone for a moment in the peering eyes, "And so no wonder I've known all my life that I would make my fortune mining. I haven't made it yet, but I will though. I'm going to make a big strike in this mountain here."

The ghostly smile hovered again as he looked at my companion, the manager of the big mine in the canyon. "The old days were the days," he said. "Nowadays those that mine go about it in a way that would make a horse laugh. Why, I remember things done in Nevada that you'll never see now," and he rambled off into tales of forgotten miners and men that had been dead for generations, of fabulous strikes and squandered millions, of copper in New Mexico, and silver in Nevada, of gold-rushes and fortunes made and lost, The smoky, ill-lit cabin seemed to be peopled with the shades of the heroes of a lost saga as the old man drifted on. He had forgotten all about us, and was living in a dead past among his dead friends. Names and places eddied vaguely around us: Sun Mountain, the Gould and Curry, Judge Turner, Virginia City,

Bill Stewart, Kern River, a thousand to the ton, Calumet …

I do not think old Jack noticed our departure when we left. He was still lost in the days when he, and the West, were young.

I went across to the town of Butte to watch Helena playing Butte at football.

Butte is without exception the least pleasing town which I have ever seen. It is worse than Gary, or Sheffield, or a Welsh mining town, or the slums of Glasgow, or anything in the Ruhr valley. Butte is uglier, and dirtier, and more blatantly sordid than any of them.

And the country round is an unspeakable desolation. In the old days of "rugged individualism," the roaring days of Butte when Heinze, the brilliant young Jew, was fighting Amalgamated Copper and Standard Oil together, anyone who pleased could set up a smelter and flood the land with sulphur fumes, and the result to-day is the barren wilderness of the mountain-slopes around Butte. No trees grow on them or grass or any living thing. It is a nightmare of a country. If you substitute the words "mountain range" for the word "plain," Browning's description of the Duke's country perfectly fits Butte and its surroundings :

… one vast red drear burnt-up plain,
Branched through and through with many a vein
Whence iron's dug, and copper's dealt;
Look right, look left, look straight before, —
Beneath they mine, above they smelt,
Copper-ore and iron-ore,
And forge and furnace mould and melt,
And so on, more and ever more …

The hill itself has a certain grim fascination. It is so completely more monstrous in its hideousness than any other hill, and at the same time so fantastic in the wealth of its minerals, that at least it possesses the quality of uniqueness. There is no other hill in the world like it, with its four thousand miles of underground workings, its unbelievable richness in gold, silver, copper, manganese, oil, and coal, and its story of the terrific seven years war that was fought in its tunnels by the miners of the rival companies.

The football game was even less like Rugby football and even more like the World War than the Princeton-Williams game. There were periods when the ball lay, neglected and ignored, upon the ground for several minutes at a time while the players discussed their outstanding differences with some violence.

And proceedings were enlivened, although enlivenment was hardly necessary, by an extremely intoxicated supporter of the Butte interest who kept on imploring the Butte team, in a terrific voice, to go back to copper-mining, and occasionally varying the appeal with the plaintive inquiry, "What's wrong with Dublin Gulch?" It appears that Dublin Gulch is a tough locality, even judged by the standards of Butte.

After the battle was over I went, with a heavy heart, to the railroad station (or was it deepo?) to catch the express for the south and leave the enchanted State of open hearts and magical blue mountains.

I had a miserable journey. The food in the Dining-Car was execrable, I had a splitting headache after so much Montanan hospitality, and as I was tossing to and fro in my bunk I remembered that I had left my hat, the only really handsome black felt hat in the whole of the United States, in the Dining-Car and that the Dining-Car was bound for Portland, Oregon, whereas I was heading for Salt Lake City.

CHAPTER TEN

Crossing the great desert, the alkaline plains, I beheld
enchanting mirages of waters and meadows.

WALT WHITMAN

Salt Lake City has fascinated me ever since I read, many, many years ago, Conan Doyle's *Study in Scarlet*, the tale of Jefferson Hope, the Latter Day Saints, the Avenging Angels, Brigham Young and the Great Alkali Plain. The fascination lay partly, I admit, in the fact that it contained the début of Mr. Sherlock Holmes. But Dr. Watson's descriptions of the Utah scene were enough to fire the imagination of any child. "The coyote skulks among the scrub," wrote the doctor, "the buzzard flaps heavily through the air, and the grizzly bear lumbers through the dark ravines, and picks up such sustenance as it can among the rocks. These are the sole dwellers in the wilderness." I used to lie awake in my nursery, thinking of the "three solemn buzzards who uttered raucous screams of disappointment and flapped sullenly away," and of the newly dug grave in the canyon on the road to Carson City, and I have been determined for years to visit the strange and famous City on the shore of the Great Salt Lake. And that, of course, was where I got my first shock, for the City is by no means on the shore of the Lake. It is a good fifteen or twenty miles away. However, the disappointment caused by that was soon compensated by the magnificence of the site of the town. Whatever the virtues or vices of Brigham Young may have been, whatever his attainments and limitations, there is one thing that can be said about him he knew where to put his City at the end of the long pilgrimage. It must have been a profoundly moving moment when the little band came struggling down Pioneers Canyon, and Young looked at the great plain in its horse-shoe of purple mountains and said, simply, "This is the place." Those four words, and his name, and the date — July 2, 1847, are all that is carved on the monument at the foot of the Canyon, and they are more impressive in their simplicity than any oratorical or classical inscription could be.

After reporting the loss of my hat to the railroad officials, I did the accepted round of the Temple buildings, listened to the perfervid description of Mormonism and its doctrines from the guide, of which I could not understand a word, heard the famous pin drop in the great Hall (and was exceedingly sceptical about the genuineness of the acoustical phenomenon) and examined, with an alarm that almost verged on terror, the hideous statues of Joseph Smith and Hyrum Smith in the Temple gardens among the dahlias, the marigolds. But the monument to the seagulls touches the heart, and the guide told us all — for by this time I had somehow got entangled in a large party of sightseers — the strange story of how the grasshoppers came and devoured the crops of the early settlers and how, in despair, the starving community prayed for Divine assistance, and how the seagulls came up in thousands from the Salt Lake and annihilated the grasshoppers. I gathered that it is a good deal safer to kill a man in Utah, even in this year of grace, nearly a hundred years after, than to shoot a seagull.

The statue of Brigham Young stands at the cross-roads outside the precincts of the Temple, and has been orientated in the true tradition of American statues. Just as Liberty has her back to America, and Orpheus at Baltimore has his back, and rightly, to the spot where Francis Scott Key wrote the unfortunately immortal "Star-Spangled Banner," so Brigham Young has his back to the Temple and his hand outstretched towards one of the local banks. Not that he need stretch out his hand to a bank. The Mormon Church needs no overdraft. Every good Latter-Day Saint voluntarily gives one-tenth of his income to the Church, and its wealth is prodigious.

I took a taxi and drove round the town and marvelled at the breadth and magnificence of its planning. They were better at town-planning in 1847, those rough hardy men, than anyone is nowadays, and the automobiles can park two deep on each side of the Main Street that Brigham Young's mathematical colleague designed, and still leave room for six or eight cars to drive abreast in between. Running water from mountain springs keeps the gutters clean, and fills the pool in Liberty Park, Brigham Young's farm that he bequeathed to the community.

Salt Lake City is a city of many memories. The wall of the Temple is on the exact line where the settlers heaped up their earth wall as a defence against the Indians in 1847; a monument on the sidewalk in Main Street marks the site of a station of the Pony Express; in the museum in the Capitol is preserved Young's covered wagon and in Liberty Park is his log-cabin and his mill; outside Young's house are the stones to which the Elders of the Church used to tie their horses when they came to the council.

But the strangest of all is Brigham Young's tomb. Remember that the Mormons are Americans and therefore not desperately anxious to retire their lights under modest bushels. Remember that they are all bursting with pride at their astonishing achievement. Remember that the money-bags of the Church are bulging with dollars. And remember that advertisement for the further expansion and glory of the Church is a ruling passion. Then, when you have got these four ideas into your head, imagine what a Mausoleum of splendour and ostentation must mark the last resting-place of the man who brought them through the wilderness and laid the foundations of the Church upon so strong a base.

You will have a job to find Young's tomb. It is in a tiny graveyard in a side-street, railed off with a low railing, guarded by a locked gate, and marked with no label or sign post. The grave itself has no name on it, and straggly, untidy creepers clamber over the massive stone slab. Some of his wives lie in the same small burial-ground. Their graves bear their, names.

Young is alone in his magnificent anonymity. Whatever he may have been in life — and controversy rages round him — in death at any rate he showed greatness by being "as content with six foot as the Moles of Adrianus." His tomb is shabby and creeper-covered, but his memorial lies all round him, the city which he made and the State which he founded.

I was standing by the anonymous stone and looking out across the smoky city — for Salt Lake is a city of coal-burners — when a voice broke in upon me.

"Were you ever in Huddersfield?" it said, unexpectedly. I turned round, and there was my taxi-driver. "I was two years on a Mission in Huddersfield and Bradford," he went on chattily. "Never enjoyed myself so much in my life."

"Mission?" I said. "What sort of Mission?"

"Why, a Mission for the Church," the taxi-driver replied, and he explained to me the system by which young Mormons go abroad for a couple of years, and preach at street corners and in villages and in highways and byways, in European cities and in Samoan islands, in Christian lands and *in partibus infidelium*, expounding the Word of the Lord as it was revealed to Joseph Smith at Palmyra on September 22, 1827.

"Do they pay your expenses?" I asked.

"No. You have to find your own expenses," said the taxi-driver, and I began to see that President Young bequeathed more to the Church than Liberty Park. For the President combined a fanatical belief in Mormonism with a very nice appreciation of the material advantages which may be found in this world, and he was able to preach his version of the Christian doctrines without being a whit worried by the scriptural injunction to sell that thou hast, and give to the poor. When Brigham Young died, he left two and a half million dollars to seventeen wives and his fifty-six children. Following dutifully in his footsteps, the Church relies on volunteer missionaries and only pays the expenses of new Saints from distant parts who are too poor to travel to Utah. The large hotel which I stayed in, and the large stores in which I did my shopping, both belonged to the Church.

It is an odd circumstance that the only thing which anyone knows about the Mormons is not true. They are not polygamists and have not been for at least forty years. But in Great Britain at any rate, even to well-educated people the word "Mormon" means a polygamist and nothing else.

I was able to reflect on all this and much more during my drive to the smelting-works and the copper-mine at Bingham. For I need hardly say that after resolutely declining to visit either of them, I was put into an automobile and driven out to visit both of them. As it turned out, the copper-mine was interesting enough, for it is not a mine at all but a solid hill side which is being steadily blasted away. Already half of it has gone and a gigantic semicircle, like a Greek theatre, has been hollowed out of the mountain. It is a most spectacular sight, for the quartz, or whatever it is, is white and the minerals in it make a dazzling display of greens and yellows and peacock-blues and golds and silvers. But, beautiful though it was, I did not dally overlong. Blasting was in full swing, and there were notices everywhere of the danger from falling stones, and the air was full of warlike sounds.

So I fled back, down the steep little street in the canyon, lined with Swiss chalets and shacks, and peopled with Italians and Greeks and Japs and Germans and Chinamen, into the safety of the dry, flat plain. As I scuttled down I caught a glimpse of a shop which advertised itself as Christ's Grocery and Sugar Stores, so the visit was not a dead loss.

Then came, of course, the usual visit to the smelter, but, curiously enough, the folks of Salt Lake City are more hospital-conscious than smelter-conscious. Every trip in an automobile which I took invariably ended up at the handsome new War-hospital on the top of the hill behind the town. I do not think my hosts were animated by any other motive than Civic Pride. Had it been a Mental Home I might have grown suspicious at the perpetually recurring visits, but I could detect no suggestion of this kind on the bland faces of my friends.

It was in Salt Lake City that I made my first contact with the Young Republican movement. I had heard, vaguely, when I was in the East, of the uprising of the youth of the shattered Republican party, but somehow the stranger in New York does not encounter very much in the big political line. New York, so far as National politics is concerned, seemed to me to be rather like London, which is politically the dullest and most apathetic community in Great Britain. But it was not until I reached Utah that I met, for the first time, young men who were burning with the fire of Crusaders, who were devoting all their spare time and energies to the two sacred Causes of overthrowing President Roosevelt and of purging Republicanism so it should become something worthy to be battled for by young men and women.

I listened for hours to young men talking. I do not say that they were especially constructive, or that they did not repeat a good many platitudes, or that they had more ideas than words. But their eyes were filled with a burning light and their hands trembled with sincerity and emotion. It seemed to me that I was listening to something new, and at the same time to something that was nearly two hundred years old, when phrases filled the air like the Bill of Rights ... We must go back to the Declaration of Independence ... Sanctity of Contracts ... the Confidence of the Governed ... Principles of true Democracy ... It is always a rash, and usually a stupid, thing for a foreigner to open his mouth when the internal politics of somebody else's country are being discussed, and so I only asked one very mild question: "Has the Young Republican movement always been like this?"

"Of course not," my young friends answered. "In the past the people who ought to have been guiding us, what you in England call the Ruling Classes, were too busy making money. They left politics to the professionals, on the sure understanding that the Republicans would always win the Presidential Election. Roosevelt has changed all that. He's given us such a jolt that we've got awake at last. In the long run, if he doesn't completely smash the country first, Roosevelt is the best friend that the Republican party has ever had. And in the long run also, Depression has been a good friend to us, though it is a bit hard to convince a busted millionaire of that. But we're all alive now, and we're going to make the Republican party the greatest political power for Good that any country has ever known."

After they had shown me their committee-rooms and given me sheaves of pamphlets, they rushed off to address meetings and organize campaigns which were to bring the inevitable, irresistible Victory to their Crusade.

I strolled back to my hotel where I found a telegram to say that my hat had been last seen passing through Portland, Oregon, and moving in a north-westerly direction, and that further bulletins would be issued later.

That evening I dined at an Italian restaurant on Main Street and was excited when I found that the wine-list offered several Sauternes, a Chablis, and a Riesling. There are many capital drinks to be made out of rye whisky, but I was sadly missing my bottle of wine at dinner. On many occasions whisky is a good drink — after the second round of golf on a winter's day, on the stone slabs of an American Bowl during a football match, on a hillside out of a tin mug in a snowstorm, or just before running through a heavy barrage of 5.9

shells in a World War, in which case it is best drunk out of the bottle — at all these times and at many others, whisky is a grand drink and has saved many a life. But to wash down a good dinner with it is a barbarous custom and one that would not have been tolerated for an instant by the claret-drinkers who first invented it and distilled it. There is one sole exception to this rule, and that is when there is nothing else to drink at all, which happened to me, as already recorded, at Billings, Montana.

It was with a loud and wine-bibulous cry, therefore, that I waved the wine-list above my head and shouted for the wine-waiter. None of the other diners paid any attention to me. Nobody ever pays any attention in America. I never met such a people in my life for minding their own business. It is positively uncanny. If I had led a pink elephant down Main Street in Salt Lake City or anywhere else, I doubt if anyone would have done more than throw a casual glance at me, and the only difference it would make to the life of the place would probably be the erection of a notice-board or two, a few hours later, saying, "Pink elephants parked here, 50 c."

The Proprietor, a charming Italian, paid attention to my cries, however, and within a moment all my hopes were dashed. For the Sauternes were Californian, and the Chablis was Californian, and the Riesling was Californian, and even the "Sparkling Moselle" was Californian. As a matter of fact they made a very pleasant drinking — I tried them all before I left the City — but they were not the wines of France or Germany. Incidentally, I never could understand why the prices of California wine are so relatively high in America. A dollar and a half is a great deal to pay for what is, after all, a wine of no international distinction. During my visit to the United States I drank quite a lot of Californian wine, but I would have drunk a great deal more if it had cost, perhaps, thirty cents a bottle, for, as I say, it is quite palatable stuff. In France they can sell local vin ordinaire at a franc and a half per litre, and a franc and a half at par is somewhere about seven cents. Surely then California could produce a vin ordinaire to sell at thirty or forty. If she did, she would gradually build up a great community of wine-drinkers who at present prefer to send five dollars (minus the revenue-duty, of course) to my native country for a bottle of Scotch, rather than a dollar and a half to California for a bottle of "Sauterne." Naturally I do not complain at the ceaseless flow of dollars into Scotland, but I think it is curious. And why on earth do they ape the European, and label their new-world wines with old-world names? There are plenty of lovely names in California, and I, for one, would sooner drink a Santa Catalina or a Monterey or a Piedra Blanca than the same wine labelled Château Yquem (Cal.) or Californian Mouton Rothschild or Domestic Hermitage.

However, it is no affair of mine.

I enjoyed Salt Lake City and its queer, earnest people. They talk a great deal, but you get the impression that they mean what they say.

And there were more pretty girls to every square yard of sidewalk in Salt Lake City than in any city I had yet visited. The town is full of them. I asked several people for the cause of this pleasing phenomenon, but each gave a different cause. One, an ardent young ex-Missioner who had recently come back from his proselytizing sojourn in foreign parts, treated it as a matter of course. The same all-protecting Deity which sent the seagulls, also sent the standard of Beauty. Another, obviously a Rationalist, put it down to the salty air from the Great Lake which, he said, produced the dazzling colouring and the lovely skins, while a third, a morose gentleman who was travelling the country in an apparently vain endeavour to sell some mechanical device for doing something or other — he explained it to me at great length in the lounge, but I did not understand a word — brightened for a moment and said, "Ah! but you should see Kentucky," and retired again behind a rampart of typescript. But whatever the cause, there is the fact. The ladies of Salt Lake City are very beautiful.

As I was leaving to catch the early morning train to Ogden, where I was to pick up the San Francisco express, a telegram was handed to me. It reported that my hat was now at the railroad junction of Pocatello, Idaho.

I changed at Ogden and was met by an excitedly tearful station official. Brandishing a dossier of official telegrams, he informed me with a sob in his throat that my hat had passed through Ogden in the small hours of the morning in the Pocatello-Salt Lake City train, and was even now lying in the station at Salt Lake.

CHAPTER ELEVEN

The flashing and golden pageant of California,
The sudden and gorgeous drama, the sunny and ample lands,
The long and varied stretch from Puget Sound to Colorado south,
Lands bathed in sweeter, rarer, healthier air, valleys and
mountain cliffs.

WALT WHITMAN

The Great Salt Lake, on a sunny morning when there is no wind, is a symphony in steel and snow. The snowy mountains come down to the very edge of it on every side, and the reflection of the snow in the water makes the steel more icily white, and the reflection of the water on the mountain sides makes the snow more steely blue. Seventy miles long and thirty across, the lake is a vast, burnished, silent sheet. There are no dark specks upon it where the fisherfolk ply their immemorial trade, for there are no fish. There are no birds to be seen and no movement of life. The salt foam piles up against the causeway for the railroad runs straight across the lake in thick yellow curls and bubbles. On every side is majesty, beauty, and utter solitude. It is a relief to reach at last the hideous, dazzling desolation of the Great American Desert, for there at least is an occasional raven, heavy and sinister, flapping hither and thither in search of something dead. It is a mystery how anything could have lived in that endless stretch of pure white sand, unbroken even by tufts of sage-grass or tumbleweed, but presumably something must have, or the raven would not have been searching for its poor body. Even this grim evidence that a living creature has passed by was somehow more cheerful than the silent deadness of the Lake. There was rather a curious incident in the dining-car that day. I was sitting alone at a table, reading the Old Testament, the best companion for a solitary journey I know, when a young lady and gentleman took their seats opposite me, and the latter informed me at once that they were honeymooning. I offered my insincerest congratulations, for I did not really care whether they were embarking upon a successful matrimonial venture or not, to which the young man replied, "You're an Englishman, whereas I'm only a crude American." I assured him that to my way of thinking he was a miracle of polish and culture, where upon he laid his head upon his girl-wife's shoulder and burst into tears. "He thinks I'm only a crude American," he kept on whimpering. "He *said* I was only a crude American." The situation was really rather ridiculous and at the same time very embarrassing. Everyone was looking at us, and the general feeling seemed to be that I had wantonly insulted a fellow passenger. I begged the youth to accept my solemn and personal affidavit that no such bower of chivalry and learning had bloomed at the court of Louis XV, that no such elegance and cosmopolitan grace had burgeoned in the Pump Room at Bath, but to no purpose. He sobbed as if his heart would break, and the word "crude" drifted round the dining-car like the crooning of a melancholy wood-pigeon. Fortunately my position and honour were retrieved by the young man himself. He rose to his feet with a kind of wobbly dignity, repeated, "I'm only a crude American," and fell flat on his back among a forest of African feet. There was a loud roar of laughter from the other lunchers and an American businessman bought me a high-ball.

The desert went on and on and on. The only change in the landscape was when a few miles of dull yellow sand lay, like a smudge left by a careless painter, across the hard white of the rest. Sagebrush, when it came at last, seemed a tropical and luxuriant vegetation, and the first gentle slopes of downland were precipitous ravines after the interminable flatness.

We slogged away through the dismal uplands of Nevada, a State that is known in Great Britain for three things only, the Comstock Lode, the pleasantly unfussy divorce-laws, and the heavy-weight fight between Jim Jeffries and Jack Johnson.

We stopped for a short time at Reno, that fabulous town of platinum blondes, but I did not descend. I ought to have, I know. For it must be a unique place, even in such a country as the United States which is full of strange places. And not so far away is the Comstock itself, and Virginia City, and the Sun Mountain. But I was tired of Metallurgy. Gold-diggers and Silver-diggers, the populations respectively of Reno and Virginia City, held small appeal for me at the moment.

I was within a yard or two of California the Golden, and I wanted sun and fruit and wine and laughter and redwood-trees, all of which I had understood from infancy were typical products of that delectable State, and I was not to be lured away by platinum heads nor deterred by the fear of earthquakes. Besides, if once I left the main routes, I would never see my hat again, the only really good black felt hat in the whole of the North American Continent. So

I missed Reno, and went westwards into the night. Next morning I would be basking in The Californian Climate. Before I climbed awkwardly on to my shelf in the Pullman that night, I re-read for the fiftieth time the exquisite opening sentence of the Railroad-Guide's description of San Francisco: "The greatness of Rome is somehow associated whether correctly or not with the fact that it was built on seven hills. How much greater, then, should San Francisco be, standing on fourteen hills?" And as I read it, I worked out the answer as I had already worked it out forty-nine times, and for the fiftieth time I got it to the same figure. The answer, so it seemed to me, surely must be, "Twice." Of course there was the possibility to be reckoned with I am not sufficiently a mathematician to decide that in assessing the historical greatness of a city according to its Coefficient of Monticulation — so to speak — one ought to work by Geometrical rather than by Arithmetical Progression. But whether that be so or not, I think that the compilers of that Railroad-Guide were lamentably deficient in the art of advertisement. Why did they stop at the comparison with Rome? Athens was built on only one hill, the Acropolis, and Troy had only Hissarlik. Is not San Francisco therefore to be reckoned as fourteen times as great as either of them, or better still, seven times as great as Athens and Troy put together? As for poor Babylon, she had no hill at all, and therefore no Coefficient of Monticulation, and therefore no greatness. Even Thomasville, Oklahoma, can beat that (at least so it appears on the bathy-orographical maps of the district).

However, let us abandon the computation of San Francisco's greatness by bathy-orographical methods, and consider it isothermally. In other words what about the Californian Climate?

When the express arrived at last, at about eight o' clock in the morning, I was tired and grimy, hungry, thirsty, and stiff from lack of exercise, and passionately longing for a bath. In ten minutes, I said to myself consolingly as I descended awkwardly and painfully from the train, I will be lying in a piping-hot bath in a large hotel, and the world will be a better place. I was wrong. I was not lying in a piping-hot bath, and the world was a much, much worse place. For it appeared very soon that San Francisco has no railroad station, at least not one that was of any use to me. We had been decanted on the other side of the bay, and had to line up and wait for a ferry-boat to take us across. A cold wind blew through the chinks in the shed where we waited. Hunger was gnawing. My fellow passengers looked as tousled and unshaven to me as I have no doubt that I looked to them, while my crude young friend sat on a bench with his head in his hands and rocked backwards and forwards, groaning most lugubriously. His eyes were pink and his face light green, and the ensemble, reminiscent as it was of some sort of vegetarian dish that has gone wrong in the cooking and is about to be thrown away, and rightly, was not at all pleasing.

When once we were aboard the ferry, a difficult problem had to be settled. For there was a small breakfast-restaurant on it, with a most delicious scent of hot coffee, and I had to decide whether to waste a ravening appetite on what might prove to be an indifferent meal but would at the same time undoubtedly allay the mordant pains from which I was suffering, or whether to carry out my original programme and resist temptation till I reached my hotel, wallow in a hot bath, shave, pick up my mail, and saunter down to a huge and succulent breakfast like a gentleman at ease. The second was the programme dictated by my head and heart. But other forces, heavily acted upon by the scent of the coffee, were at work and in a sudden abandon of voracity I turned towards the restaurant. At that precise moment a torrent of young, pretty, chattering girls came swirling on to the ferry-boat and in a twinkling every seat in the restaurant was occupied; about three deep, by commuters. By this time my whole internal mechanism was tuned up for the reception of that coffee, and there was nothing for me to do but to lean over the bulwark and swear comprehensively at the Cosmos from the stars in their courses, down via San Francisco, to the humblest commuter on the ferry.

My one consolation was the weather. The wind was colder than ever. A thick mist was beating up across the bay, and it was raining hard. It would have been a bad day on the north-east coast of Scotland at the time of the mid-winter gales.

That afternoon three San Franciscan friends invited me to play golf with them at the Berkeley Country Club. It was a very interesting experience. I have played golf at many places for a number of years, but never before have I tried to swing a club and at the same time suppress volleys of Homeric laughter. For we played round the course in a thick white fog, and on almost every tee one or other of my charming hosts would say, "On an ordinary day you can see forty-eight miles from here," or "This is the first time in twenty-seven years that I haven't seen sixty-six miles from this spot," or "This is our best view of all," and I would peer diligently into the fog and try very hard not to laugh and enquire politely in what approximate direction I ought to strike the ball now. Throughout that round I never saw forty-eight feet or sixty-six feet in any direction, let alone miles. But looking back on it afterwards, I wondered whether, in not laughing at my first experience of the Californian climate, I displayed any greater heroism than my hosts in not crying.

Next day we played again, and the fog had lifted and the sun was shining and all the supreme panorama was spread out at our feet, but somehow I felt that I had got a hold on California for the rest of my life and that, however great her glories, however high her destiny, she would never be able to look me squarely in the face.

The three harbours of San Francisco, Sydney, and Rio de Janeiro, are among the most powerful instruments of boredom which the globe-trotter wields. A fourth used to be Niagara, but ever since Oscar Wilde spoke of it with such marked discourtesy, it has been, by tacit consent, allowed to sublapse from the polite tittle-tattle of the ship's lounge. But the harbours remain rampant examples of the devastating effect of anything beautiful in Nature upon the souls of the globe-trotters. And the irritating thing about San Francisco, at any rate, is that everything which these semi-literate pests can say in praise of its harbour, can only be an understatement. It is the most beautiful thing that I have seen in my life. I stood on that second evening on the heights of Berkeley and looked across to the sunset which was splashing the Pacific with all the colours in the paint box.

Long shadows, and a heat-haze, and a faintly rising mist, and the sunset, all confused and blurred the sharp outlines of the harbour below us, so that wooded promontories seemed to merge with the water, and you could not tell where the hills began and the reflections began, and the islands shimmered like mirages, and the tiny waves wandered lazily into tree-fringed bays, and the air seemed to be full of rose-coloured dust that glowed against the clouds of the sunset.

Sailing boats were scattered on the harbour like sleepy butterflies and sometimes a curl of slow smoke marked the passage of a steamer in another, unseen corner of the immense anchorage. For the immensity of it is overwhelming. Looking down we could see miles and miles of the land-locked bay, stretching out here in a long, unbroken sheet of water, vanishing there behind an island, reappearing suddenly far inland, almost behind us, fading yonder into the sky, or the Pacific, or both, and yet we could not see the main part of the harbour, where the big ships ply up to berth and the floating caravans come in from the Orient, and San Francisco itself was invisible.

Not every trace of man's handiwork, however, was invisible to us. The hills away to the north were plentifully scattered with huge and hideous oil-tanks belonging to some oil-company, and nearer, the suburb of Richmond is high in the tradition of New Jersey's worst achievements, with a full complement of railroads, steel-bridges, pylons, and straggly, ill-planned building development.

I strolled back along the golf-course, bright with wild orange eschscholtzias, and sniffed the aromatic spicy scent of burning eucalyptus wood, and then drove down through the terraces of gay villas, beflowered, even in the late November, with violas and petunias and nasturtiums and camassias, and garlanded with bougainvillaea, and on sea-level I found another beautiful example of America's above-ground traction. Built, I should think, about 1770, five or six mammoth scarlet cars clank gaily down the middle of the road for miles and miles to the ferry where I had suffered so much on the previous day. In high good humour, partly conduced by the golf, partly by the harbour and the sunset and the flowers, partly by the street-railway (always a certain winner with me), and partly by the turkey, plum-pudding, rye, and quite admirable liqueur with which my host in Berkeley had regaled me, I returned to my hotel and found that a very important change had taken place during my absence. I had been elected an honorary member of the famous Bohemian Club and had been invited to occupy a suite of rooms in the Club's magnificent new building. From this moment my life in San Francisco became lost in a sort of oriental dream of splendour. I have a vague recollection of thick carpets, and deep arm chairs, and swift and silent service, and wonderful food, and universal kindness. I remember leaning up against the bar in one of the largest bar-rooms I have ever seen (it would have restored Michael Finsbury's confidence in the human race), and I remember begging vainly to be allowed to pay for a drink just once, so as not to carry away with me the remorse of a hundred-per-cent sponger. And I remember being shown the very fine mural paintings of the celebrated Redwood Grove, which were at the time nearing completion. But all the rest is merged into an imperial haze in which I seemed to be playing the part of Haroun-al-Rashid.

The picture-laden walls of the lordly bar point to the number of distinguished artists who are members of the Bohemian Club, and the annual dramatic productions in the Grove to the distinguished dramatists and actors, and the brilliant conversation to the wits and poets. But I could not help feeling that the word "Bohemian" has travelled almost as far from the Vie de Bohème, with its poverties, its garrets, its squalors, its despairs, as the distance between the Golden Gate and the Quartier Latin. Indeed I felt that probably I was the only member (for such was I for a glorious, unforgettable week) who was really qualified for membership according to the definition of "Bohemian" in the *New English Dictionary*: "An artist, literary man, or actor, who leads a free, vagabond, or irregular life, not being particular as to the society he frequents, and despising conventionalities generally. (Used with considerable latitude, with or without reference to morals.)", though of course the clubmen might reply that it was pretty clear that at least they were not particular as to the society they frequented. But against that, I was unquestionably the only member, permanent or temporary, who did not possess a hat.

Having settled down into my Caliphal residence, I started out to explore the city.

The first thing that strikes the stranger in San Francisco is that it is built not upon fourteen hills but upon about ten thousand ladders. I never saw such streets. Wherever you turn, a street is either plunging down into an abyss below you or climbing vertically into the heavens above you. Occasionally you come to a transverse street and then you get the impression that you are standing on a shelf, half-way up the wall of a gargantuan room or on one of those narrow ledges in the Rocky Mountains, with a precipice on one side and a sheer cliff on the other, on which the young, curly-haired hero of our boyhood-tales invariably used to encounter a grizzly bear while flying from a band of hostile Sioux. These straight-up-and-down ladders are simply fantastical in their steepness. The street-cars will not trust themselves to electricity upon such giddy drops, but cling passionately to a creaking cable. But even these streets are not the most preposterous in the town, for there is one that is nothing more or less than a spiral staircase, broad enough to take an automobile. You go whirling round and round, with your car tilted to an angle of about sixty degrees, your engine boiling, your ears singing, and your head swimming. Coming down is even worse, for you spin down like a crazy fly on a cork screw, expecting every moment to fall off and lie at the bottom with your legs kicking in the air.

I found it less dizzy, and less tiring to the ankles, to keep to the lower part of the city. Fisherman's Wharf, for instance, is a pleasant spot to while away an hour. The little fishing-boats, blue and green and yellow and brown, lie at their moorings in the basin, and Italian urchins howl imprecations at one another, and the gulls, with proud hook-noses like early Roman Emperors, stand on the tops of the warehouses, and the fattest, sleekest, smuggest, blandest cats roll from one fish-stall to another, disdaining anything lower in the piscine hierarchy than a fresh lobster, and the stalls are covered with strange-looking fish and sea-shells diapered with all the colours of the celestial prism.

The Barbary Coast is a disappointment, for it is only a memory. Its horrific days of fame and iniquity are over, and its windows are broken and boarded up, and its dwelling places are the haunt of the spider and the cockroach. But Chinatown is still with us, and to Chinatown in San Francisco, as to Harlem in New York, I made my pilgrimage. It was an interesting experience, but more interesting for its suggestion of hidden mysteries, of an age-old life no European or American will ever see, of a world that lives and loves and works and plays behind a veil that is eternally impenetrable, rather than what we actually saw. The façade for the tourist is a hundred times more cleverly disguised than the tawdry façade at Harlem, and everywhere there is a dignity and orderliness that comes from ten thousand years of knowledge. But it is only a façade. The life of Chinatown is not for passing travellers. We were shown the Hall of the Four Families with its pictures and its tapestries and carvings and metal-work and carpets, but after we had seen and admired them all, we were no nearer to an understanding of the Four Families and the beneficent power which they have wielded wherever Chinese are gathered together, ever since the four became bound in friendship in the century that we call the seventh B.C.

We stood in the middle of the Chinese theatre and watched the gaily dressed actors intoning their parts, and listened to the incessant clashing discords of the orchestra which seem to be more important to the action than anything which the players say or do, and marvelled at the delicate, porcelain beauty of an actress who was preparing to go on, and looked at the hundreds and hundreds of boxes containing dresses and "props"; and at the end I felt that I understood just as much about the Chinese Theatre as I did about the Chinese newspaper which I went to see being "put to bed" later on in the evening.

I went to the Hall of the Six Companies and listened to an exposition in perfect English of who the Companies are and what they mean, and at the end I felt that I had been listening to a ghost.

Chinatown in San Francisco is full of colour and picturesque-ness and beauty and glamour. But all that we see is just a show staged with gentle decorum to satisfy a lot of little children whose countries had never been heard of when Confucius was teaching philosophy to an ancient nation. The Show is perfectly arranged. There is no hint of patronage to spoil the self-esteem of the children. Meticulous care is taken to see that no infantile feelings are hurt, and at the end of the tour dolls and other toys, sticks of incense, carved toy-temples, embroidery, bronze Buddhas, little souvenirs of a happy evening, are distributed among the tiny tots, at a purely nominal cost, by the grave and courteous seniors. The children clutch their treasures, thank their entertainers with a becoming diffidence, bob and curtsey, and scuffle off home. Their entertainers put up the shutters, and snuff out the lights, and vanish gravely into the darkness. They are free at last, after a long evening, to go to Chinatown.

When I got back to the Bohemian Club that night, I found a square cardboard box awaiting me. It was of a size large enough to contain a wedding-cake of grandiose construction, and it was corded and sealed like a dispatch-box. Inside it were layers and layers of paper, and, nestling snugly at the core of it all, was my hat. Its single-handed odyssey was over at last, and once again I was the best-hatted man in all America.

I went down to Monterey, the old Pacific capital, to see the house in which Robert Louis Stevenson lived before he went to Samoa. We motored there on a day of mingled loveliness and tension, and the unfair thing was that I had all the loveliness and none of the tension, whereas my hosts were situated exactly the other way round. For it was the day of the elections, November 6th, and California was in a sad turmoil. Utopia was just round the corner, it appeared, and Utopia, as so often happens in this crazy world, inevitably meant ruin for all that is brightest and gayest. The ancient regime of California, with all its wit, its elegance, its culture, its careless charm, was hearing the distant creak of the tumbrils and seeing the distant surge of the red Phrygian caps. If the corner was turned at the election and the party of Utopia proved victorious, then all that ancient régime would be swept away by the mob to the economic and financial lamp post. No wonder that on that sixth of November there was tension in the air. But the only effect that the political crisis had upon me, the Bohemian, "the vagabond of irregular habits," was the ordinance that no drinks should be sold before seven P.M. on the day of the election. My hosts, preoccupied with the possibility that the next twenty-four hours might see them engulfed in irremediable ruin, had forgotten all about this dry ordinance, and when I produced, at 11.30 A.M., a bottle of good Scotch whisky from my overcoat pocket, my stock went up prodigiously, and with one accord we dismissed Utopia from our minds for the rest of the day.

That drive from San Francisco to Monterey was unforgettable. For many miles our road lay along a wooded ridge with the fertile Californian Valley below us on the left, cosy, rich, peaceful, and on our right the Pacific, shimmering in an early morning haze of sun light and vapour that made the blue of the ocean very pale and delicate. We went on and on through the woods, and the mounting sun set on fire the red bark of the madrone trees and the grey squirrels danced in the tops of the eucalyptus trees, and the air was so full of the scents of the juniper and the myrtle that I could shut my eyes and believe that I was in my native Scotland, and that the eternal roll of the deep organ-note was the Atlantic breaking upon the islands, and not the Pacific upon the old Spanish coast.

It was with deep misgivings that I approached the Redwood trees, for our route lay through one of the Groves, because they are among the Wonders of the World which have had their full share of Publicity. Every Californian, all the world over, regards himself or herself as an honorary full-time publicity agent for the Redwoods, and is never backward with statistics, comparisons, and fully adjectived descriptions. In consequence the rest of the world has rather got into the habit of automatically connecting in its mind a train of thought which runs something like this: "Here is a Californian — Climate — Redwoods — twenty-minutes speech — opportunity for a nice sleep." And forty winks are thereupon snatched.

But I need not have been afraid. There is no anti-climax. The Redwoods win. They are unbelievably impressive, far, far more impressive than anything I had expected. Even the most eloquent and imaginative Californian — and I have met many who were richly endowed with both eloquence and imagination — cannot adequately convey the sense of majesty and mystery that surround these trees. The God of the Redwood forests is not Pan, the dancing, pipe-playing, goat-footed, Puck-nosed little Arcadian, frightening wayfarers with his irresponsible shouts, but Dodonian Zeus himself, Father of the Olympian Gods, the Gatherer of Clouds, the High Thunderer, whose altar stood among the great mountain trees of Epirus.

But I do not propose to join the Californian patriots in their gallant attempt upon the impossible. The theme is too stupendous.

Those selfsame trees, under which we stood that morning, were a thousand years old when Cleopatra was reigning in Egypt. They were strong young trees when Helen was sailing across the Aegean Sea to Troy, and as seedlings they knew that unparalleled day, never again to be repeated in all their long meteorological experience, when "the sun stood still in the midst of heaven, and hasted not to go down about a whole day" in order to enable Joshua the more effectively to smite the Amorites.

We lunched on the way to Monterey in a restaurant that deserves an honourable mention for its remarkable interior. In fact I never saw anything like it in my life. It was in the middle of a pine-wood, but no clearing had been cut in the trees for it, Trees, rocks, shrubs, had all been left untouched, and the four walls simply built round them. A small stream tinkled pleasantly through the dining-room, with miniature cataracts and pools, and flowers grew on its banks. The tables were dotted about among the pines. In fact all the amenities contributed by Nature to the restaurant were charming. Man's efforts to imitate them with Ye olde Rustick woodworke were not so good. Indeed Man's idea of what God would have done with the business of Creation, if only He had had the good fortune to take a College degree in fretwork, is often a little naïve.

As we came near to Monterey the scent of the Ocean, which had never been absent from the air for long at a time all that day, even in the depths of the redwood-groves, grew more and more pungent, and the roll and boom of the surf muttered and rumbled in front of us. Robert Louis spoke a true word when he said that at Monterey the ocean is the all-pervading presence. "A great faint sound of breakers follows you high up into the inland canons, the roar of water dwells in the clean, empty rooms of Monterey as in a shell upon the chimney; go where you will you have but to pause and listen to hear the voice of the Pacific."

All Americans who wring their hands at the new-ness of their country ought to be compelled to make a pilgrimage to a number of old cities in the United States, and one of them most certainly ought to be the old Pacific capital. Monterey could teach them several things. There are layers of civilization in Monterey. Modernity, of course, is represented in a large hotel. But just round the corner there is the first house that was ever built of brick in California, and not far is the first theatre, a small, low, white house, gaily decorated with geraniums and petunias. Its date is interesting, 1847, two years before the gold-rush. The gold-miners did not bring all the licentiousness with them. Stevenson's house is a simple, two-storied building, whitewashed, with a pleasant ornamentation along the top under the rain-gutter, and a tablet recording that R. L. S. lived there in 1879.

Earlier than any of these is the Custom House, which dates from 1814, built of adobe and roofed with red tiles during the last tottering years of the mainland Empire of Spain. But the oldest of all is the long white building which was the Headquarters of General José Castro while he was "Military Commandant of the Northern Department" many a score of years ago. Here is the authentic link between Cortez and Pershing, a fragment of history, an echo of a romantic past. And how do the Americans treat this national monument? Is it a Museum? Has it been bought by a millionaire and presented to the Nation? Is it treasured by a people who spend so much time deploring that they have so little to treasure? Not on your life. Part of it is a printing-press and part of it is a saddle- shop. At the back, the white adobe wall that surrounded the Spanish Bear-Pit is crumbling to dust. Weeds and rubbish lie heavily upon it. All is in decay. And no one cares. No one pays the slightest attention. The hundred-year-old house in which a Scottish author lived for a month or two is preserved with zeal. Naturally I do not complain about that. I wish I could believe that the hotel in which I dined will be regarded in 1980 with equal veneration. But where is the sense in making such a fuss of Stevenson's temporary lodging and yet allowing a few yards away, a priceless relic of America's past to tumble into irretrievable ruin? Is America so rich in medieval Spanish Bear-Pits and remember that the Spaniards came to the neighbourhood of Monterey before 1550 — that she can afford to throw one of them recklessly away? If it comes to that, are there many medieval Spanish Bear-Pits anywhere in the world, including Spain itself? Unless something is done, and done quickly, the adobe walls will vanish, and the Bear-Pit will pass out of human memory and, sooner or later, the Headquarters itself of the Military Command of the Northern Department will join its General in the eternity of oblivion.

I wandered round the Harbour and watched the Italian fishermen mildly busying themselves on their bright-coloured boats in the evening sunlight, visited Carmel, where the artistic colony has succeeded, as artistic colonies do wherever they settle, in making a quiet place into a garish and self-conscious one, and motored back to San Francisco after dinner. We went back by a different route, across miles and miles of mud-flats that were covered with sagebrush and water and mist. Interminable processions of iron pylons marched beside us and across us and round us, bestriding the land in every direction. For a short while the *Macon*, that unfortunate airship, hovered overhead before it vanished into the gathering shadows.

Next day we learnt that California had decided not to experiment with Utopia, and faces that on the day before had been long and pale, were now round, rosy, and beaming. The votes kept on coming in all day from outlying parts of the State, but after the first excitement was over when it was incorrectly reported that Universal Wealth and happiness had carried San Francisco by the length of a street it was obvious that Universal Poverty and Misery (or whatever the ticket was called) was a popular winner.

The results as they came in, were posted in shop-windows, and I saw in one of them the saddest election result that I have ever seen. The votes in Precinct 83 had just been counted and the two leading protagonists had scored about four hundred and three hundred respectively. Then came:

Sam Darcy (Comm.), 1 vote.
Milen Dempster (Soc.), 1 vote.

I longed, quite unreasonably, for the knowledge would not have been of the slightest profit to me, to know whether Mr. Darcy voted for himself, and Mr. Dempster for himself, or whether they decided that this would be a piece of arrogance hardly in keeping with the fine old traditions of the Left Wing in American politics, and therefore agreed to vote for each other. But there was no one whom I could ask about the difficult problem, for none of my friends seemed to be either Communist or Socialist, and I hardly liked to appear to my Republican friends as one taking even an academic interest in the Left, and now I do not suppose that I shall ever know. It is a pity.

Day followed day, and still I lingered in San Francisco. My famous Itinerary had been torn up, my schedule had been thrown to the winds. Of all the cities I have ever visited, San Francisco is the most difficult to leave. Getting to it, thanks to that infernal ferry system and absence of railroad stations, is hard enough. Getting away is practically impossible.

There is a gaiety in the air that is irresistible. The street-corners are piled high with flowers on open-air stalls, and the women are more beautiful even than in Salt Lake City and dressed with a more elegant "chic" than anything which either Park Avenue or Macy's can show, and there is an atmosphere, even on the foggiest days, of sunshine. The truth, I suppose, is that San Francisco is a metropolis. It is not a provincial city looking to the Atlantic Coast for its culture, but a metropolis with its own traditions, its own ancestors, its own heritage of Spain and of the Pioneers, its own proud consciousness of history and culture. That is why it has a carefree look about it. There is no inferiority complex about San Francisco. And there is no parochialism either. At a dinner table you will hear English party politics discussed with a vast deal more understanding than you will ever hear American party politics discussed in England. In the reading-room of the Pacific Union Club you will find a file not only of the London *Times*, but of at least half a dozen British weekly papers as well, that you might search for in vain in many New York clubs.

And, of course, there is that incredible, that inescapable harbour. Day after day I requested my sixth or seventh valet at the Bohemian Club to pack my belongings and then went out for a last look at the harbour, and day after day I came back a few hours later and requested the sixth or seventh valet to unpack again. I just wanted to see once more the sun setting beyond the Golden Gate.

I used to sit for hours on the top of the hill near the Presidio and watch the steamers plugging through the fast-running currents of the Golden Gate, and the tall ferry-boats, triple-decked like oarless galleys, gliding across the harbour, like stately dames moving through the paces of an antique dance, and the soldiers drilling lazily below.

The whole fantasy of America is in that mighty panorama, the majesty and the absurdity, the vast impressiveness and the comic triviality, the quality of eternity and the quality of an urchin. Whoever doubts that America is the land of Contrasts, so startling that you do not know whether to laugh or to cry, or simply to disbelieve your own eyes, should sit with me for an hour above the Presidio. I would show him a thing or two. Firstly, I would have brought him up to our post of observation past the oldest house in San Francisco, the Commandant's house in the Presidio, built in 1776 and headquarters of Spanish, Mexican, and American rule. It is an adobe house, and a National Monument, and the San Franciscans have demonstrated with clarity that they are not careless and neglectful, like the Montereyans with their Bear-Pit. They are not going to let weeds and rubbish clutter up their oldest house. Not they. Instead, they have renovated it and painted it and tinkered it, until it looks exactly the same, and just as poisonously ugly, as any other of the barrack-square houses of the garrison. Then I would point down to the outline of the bay, and to the hideous piers of the new iron bridge which is going to stride across that loveliest of scenes. I would show him the three islands with their lovely Spanish names, Angel and Yerba Buena and Alcatraz, and tell him that Yerba Buena is often called Goat Island. I do not know whether the Spanish words mean "Good Temper," or "White Hellebore," or "Lemon-Scented Aloysia" — for my dictionary is dubiously impartial on the subject and gives all three — but I do know that, whichever they mean, the words make a more euphonious sound than "Goat." An acquaintance of mine discovered, in the old files of a San Francisco newspaper, a poem written in the form of an "Invocation to the Spirit of the Harbor," and it contained this immortal couplet:

Three islands on thy bosom float
Angel, Alcatraz, and Goat.

But the American Demon of Incongruity does not stop at renaming the magic island of the White Hellebore (or Good Temper, or Lemon-Scented Aloysia) with that ridiculous name. It has got a far better joke than that up its sleeve. For Alcatraz, tiny jewel in a perfect setting, is used as a Federal Penitentiary for some of the most hideous scoundrels that ever lived. So, my friend, as you sit beside me and gaze upon the enchanted scene, if you try to conjure up in your romantic mind the Oceanides or Nymphs of Ocean, or Hamadryads from the wooded slopes of Point Bonita, or Naiads from the ripples of the Sacramento River, you are much more likely to get a vision of a Sicilian vice-racketeer, a shot-gun in one hand and a Thompson sub-machine gun in the other, who has committed fifty atrocious murders and is serving, in consequence, a long sentence for having defrauded the Revenue of its due share of his vice profits. The sight of that little haunt of horror went far towards spoiling the bay for me. After some kind friend had explained to me what it was as I am so kindly explaining to you now I could not look at the view without my eyes being irresistibly attracted towards Alcatraz, so that in the end I almost persuaded myself that I could see a foul miasma rising from it into the air, as if the island really was a witch's cauldron in which unspeakable things were being brewed. Then I would show you, if your patience was not yet exhausted, the glorious site which is occupied by the barracks and drill-ground, and the azalea blossoms beside concrete gun-emplacements, and the shell-magazines among the eucalyptus trees, and the sentries strolling about among the palms, ready to give instant warning, presumably in the event of a surprise landing of Japanese cavalry upon the Seal Rocks. And then I would take you home past the last surviving building of the Fair of 1915, a sad stucco palace, the colour of ripened wheat, standing forlornly on the edge of an artificial lake. It looks as if it had been designed by a decorator of wedding-cakes who had once, years ago, seen a picture postcard of a Greek Temple and had tried to reproduce it from memory. The melancholy of the scene was deepened by a solitary gondola, which had once been white but was now a mottled grey, lying on its side upon a mud-bank in the lake. Greco-stucco splendour had faded, and the Carnaval de Venise was a ghost.

But the crowning joke is that San Francisco is going to restore the whole thing, temple, lake, gondola, and all, to its former magnificence.

But I tore myself away at last from the Siren City, from its parks, its museums, its Aquarium, its Exhibition of stuffed birds (in the city of St. Francis), its boulevards, its lovely and merry-minded citizens, and from the sunsets, the shadows lengthening across the Pacific, and the murmur of the breakers upon the shore.

CHAPTER TWELVE

Why this is indeed a show — it has called the dead out of
the earth!

WALT WHITMAN

I now come to the most painful experience or rather series of experiences of my entire visit to the United States of America. Looking back on it from a distance of time and thank Heaven of space also, I can still feel the horror of the nightmare. The hot breath of the Apocalyptic Horsemen is on my neck, and I still wake up on occasions in peaceful England, cold with terror from the dream that I am once again upon the road to Los Angeles.

This is what happened. A young American friend of mine offered to drive me down from San Francisco to Los Angeles in his automobile. I accepted — poor silly creature — with grateful alacrity. The alternatives were the train, with which I was getting bored, and the aeroplane, of which I have always been afraid; and so the prospect of a pleasant couple of days, dawdling down the Pacific Coast, was alluring. Even when we were breakfasting together in San Francisco, at seven A.M. on the day of our start, my young friend and I, an obvious hint of what was ahead of me was dropped, but I, still wrapped in a fool's Paradise and a European's idea of motor-travelling, hardly noticed it, let alone treated it seriously.

"We'll be there in time for dinner", remarked my friend (whom for simplicity's sake I will henceforth call Louis). Knowing the distance to be about 480 miles, I ignored such a flippant excursion into the spheres of unreality, and continued my breakfast. Even when Louis added casually that he regularly did the trip in less than twelve hours, I did not awake to the seriousness of the situation. We started off at about 7.30 A.M. and bowled out on to the splendid road to San José. At first the pace was the ordinary moderate speed to which I had become accustomed in America. That is to say, we seldom dropped below sixty and never rose above seventy. It was a glorious morning. The sun was shining, the sky was blue, the air was crisp, and although I was sad at leaving San Francisco, there was at least the small measure of consolation that is afforded by the perennial thrill of being on the road again, and heading for new country. I lay back in my seat, stretched my legs out, carolled a stave or two and gazed vacuously at the heavens or at the landscape. But after San José I began to feel a perceptible change. The wind was blowing a little harder, the note of the horn was a little more shrill, and the rest of the traffic seemed to be moving a little more slowly when it was going in the same direction as ourselves and a little more quickly when it was coming towards us. At first I was a little drowsy and did not appreciate the significance of these small changes. But when, in the middle of a yawn, I glanced at the speedometer and saw that we were moving at about ninety miles per hour I sat up abruptly. From that moment I had no more peace. Louis's jaw was stuck out, his eyes were flashing, and he crouched over his wheel like a dark demon. It was a terrifying experience. Louis did not let up for an instant. If ever he felt that he was losing his dash he would switch on the radio and the thunder of Tannhäuser or the blood-exciting music of Carmen would spur him to still more dreadful excesses of locomotion. The landscape whizzed past us, and out of many scores of miles between San José and San Luis Obispo I have no recollection of anything except the wide, tree-filled stony bed of the Salinas River.

If we crossed that river once, we must have crossed it a dozen times, backwards and forwards, from east to west and from west to east, and, for all I know, from northeast by east to southwest by west and back again. We crossed it on long steel bridges and on massive concrete bridges, on suspension bridges and on sextuple spans, on viaducts and cantilevers, on cast-iron, wrought-iron, tubular, lattice-girder, and quadrangular-girder bridges, in short on every variety of bridge known to man except the Peruvian rope-bridge of the style of San Luis Rey. And the extraordinary thing was that not once did I see a drop of water in the Salinas River. However, I was not surprised. I was long past surprise by this time, or indeed any emotion whatsoever except terror. I cannot even remember where we stopped for lunch. All I know is that Louis said we could easily lunch in seventeen minutes, and that the restaurant sold no form of stimulant stronger than coffee.

A welcome halt was at the old Spanish Mission-house of San Miguel Arcángel, a late eighteenth century building, adobe with red tiles, standing on the highway that is called El Camino del Rey to this day. We pulled the clapper-rope of an old greenish silvery bell that stood outside the door, and a Franciscan came out and showed us round. There was a small museum with a number of relics of the old Hispano-Indian days, cooking utensils, metal-work, and so on, but by far the most interesting things were the frescoes on the wall of the Chapel. They were painted by Indians with Indian materials, but presumably under the general directions of the Franciscans. For instance the Madonna is Nuestra Señora de Guadalupe, but the face is a face of an Indian woman, and the abstract decorations, in faded blues and greens and pinks, never came from the brush of a countryman of Velázquez. The bell which we rang was made of silver from the mines of Peru and was one of a chain of mission-bells on the Highway of the King from San Francisco Solano in the north to San Pedro y San Pablo on the Mexican border.

I tried to linger among the almond trees in the Mission garden, but the demon driver was impatient to be on his way again. We had wasted nearly twenty minutes as it was. There are one or two curious features about motor-driving in the United States, and, during this maniacal rush down the Pacific Coast, I had an occasional opportunity, in the brief intervals between prayers, oaths, gasps, thank-offerings for unbelievable escapes, and vows of future libations to St. Christopher, of considering them. For instance, there is far less ill-temper upon American roads than upon European. Heaven knows there is far more cause for ill-temper in America, for the things which drivers do to one another would lead to a widespread epidemic of assassination if they were done in Europe. The only rule seemed to be that the automobile with its nose in front — even if it is only an eighth of an inch — goes ahead and the rest put their brakes on. A car coming out of a farm-lane on to a giant highroad with six rows of racing automobiles flashing past, has only to push out in front of a triple string and the whole traffic has to pull up for it. So long as it is in front, that seems to be good enough. The triple string jams on its brakes, waltzes all over the road, turns somersaults, whizzes round in circles, and nobody seems to mind. There is very little swearing and hardly any horn-blowing. If you did a thing like that in England you would hear some surprising things about yourself, the air would be shattered with infuriated screeches from electric horns, and probably a retired lieutenant-colonel would bounce up from somewhere and take your name and address to prosecute you for dangerous driving. If you did it in France the leading trio of the triple string would hit you fore, aft, and amidships, and the remainder of the main-road traffic would race unconcernedly over the debris. In Germany you would, of course, spend most o the rest of your life in a Nazi dungeon. But in America nothing happens at all. The main stream pulls up. You amble across. The main stream goes on again. Another peculiar feature about the road-traffic is the Speed-Cop. His duty in life is to cruise about the roads whithersoever the spirit moves him in order to check the monstrous speed-excesses of people like Louis. And he has my warmest good-will in his task. For this purpose he is mounted upon a high-powered motorcycle. Now America is a land of fast cheap motor-cars and, in consequence, motorcycles are very uncommon. When it is possible to buy a very fine car for a handful of dollars, no one is going to ride upon a motorcycle unless it is given away with a drink of Coca Cola or enclosed in a packet of chewing-gum. When, therefore, the speed-lunatics see a motorcycle in the far distance, they are safe to assume that the odds are about fifteen to one that it is bestridden by a Speed-Cop, and accordingly they slacken speed from ninety miles an hour to a demure seventy. There is a further protection for the law-breaker. The Speed-Cop's machine is painted white and it is thereby the more clearly distinguishable at a distance. In fact the only real danger of being seized by the Law is when you come suddenly on one of its representatives round a corner. But that happens seldom. All too seldom.

Motoring in America provides one of the very few examples of an American word or expression being shorter than the corresponding English one. Mr. G. K. Chesterton has pointed out in an immortal poem how the American hustler has to say "elevator" because he hasn't time to say "lift," and "apartment" for "flat," and so on. And in motoring, at first the American ran true to form by saying "gasoline" instead of "petrol." But then some genius came along, almost certainly an Englishman, who pointed out that "gasoline" could be shortened to "gas," and after a few years of careful deliberation and methodical study of the proposition, the American nation agreed that in all probability, without prejudice, and subject to the final decision of the Supreme Court, the word "gas" might be conceded to be a shorter word than "gasoline," and so it was adopted throughout the land with extreme reluctance and misgiving.

As we hurled ourselves southwards, I could see, in the momentary gaps between the towns, that the vegetation was becoming more and more tropical. Palms were taller and cactus more hideous. Poinsettias were splashing the countryside with their gorgeous flames, and for the first time I saw the graceful leaves and crimson berries of the pepper-tree. Lemon-groves and bougainvillaea and blue plumbago and yellow-flowered acacias did their gaily coloured best to distract me from the demon-driver and his hazards, and here and there clusters of oil-derricks ruined the view of the Pacific. The small towns of California are just as ugly as the small towns in any part of the Middle West, and consist, so far as one can see, solely of Gasoline-Pumps and Advertisements. Occasionally a two- storied wooden house peeps coyly over the top of a mammoth billboard, but as a general rule it is practically impossible to detect the lairs to which the populace creeps after its long day spent in contemplation of pictorial vulgarity. Oddly enough, the American advertiser makes very little use of Sex-Appeal in his assaults upon the Public Fancy. It is very rare to see pictures of bathing nymphs, or long silk legs, or classical studies of Aphrodite, or deep-bosomed Junos, or the Rape of the Sabine Women, or ladies clad only in suspender-belts, or Cleopatra's sultry languor upon a divan, such as are the delight of his English colleague. In America an automobile, let us say a Spoffin Super-Six, is usually advertised by a huge announcement which simply says "Spoffin Super-Six is the Best," or else by a picture of the car itself, whereas in England its merits will be conveyed to the world by a girl in shorts and a brassière, and with unbelievably long legs, gazing out across the Bay of Naples.

The American small town, in effect, is a mass of slogans on boards and practically nothing else. And when you come to think of it, this plastering of the rural hamlets with exhortations to purchase this or that is a very poor example of the business acumen of the American. For if the hamlet is as completely deserted as it appears to be, it is obvious that local custom will be non-existent. While if the slogans are designed to attract the eye of the passing motorist, again the labour is in vain. For the passing motorist passes so very quickly that he sees nothing but a smudge of blaring colour, and in a moment more he is out into the countryside without the faintest recollection of what he has been implored to purchase. Of course there are the hitch-hikers who have plenty of leisure to study the slogans as they amble past, but so far as I could judge from their appearances, these gentlemen seemed unlikely to be in a position to buy goods in any considerable quantity.

Hour after hour we rushed southwards, and any faint hope that I may have cherished that Louis might relax the giddy speed as he grew tired, steadily waned. If anything he drove faster and faster as it began to dawn upon him that he had a very good chance of beating his previous record for the course. And then, just as I had given up all thought of ever seeing my native country again, hope flared up. For a sign post, of which I was able to catch a glimpse as Louis slowed down for an instant to seventy miles an hour so as not to assassinate an elderly pedestrian, told me that we were approaching the City of the Patron Saint and Protectress of all artillerymen, and I knew that I, an old gunner of the World War, was in the safe keeping of the Blessed Barbara. The sun came out as we ran merrily into the bright broad streets of the town, and the cheerful colours of the Spanish houses competed with the flowers and the flags and the streamers to give us a triumphal entry. There was high festival that day in Santa Barbara for some reason or other, and I was determined to join in, if only for half an hour, to get a rest from the demon-driver. Threatening, therefore, to brain Louis with a spanner if he did not halt, I compelled him to drive to an Olde Englyshe Tudor Hostelrie, complete with beer-mugs, bogus timbers, pictures of hunting scenes with the Belvoir and the Quorn, portraits of Mr. Pickwick, and cosy little inglenooks, where I spent one of the brightest half-hours of my life, restoring my shattered nerves, pouring libations to Santa Barbara, fortifying myself against the last lap in the journey, and resolutely preventing Louis from touching anything stronger than the beverage which in America is called, for some reason, beer. So mellow, indeed, did I become and so forgiving, that I solemnly withdrew my prayer to the Lady of Cannons that Louis should be served as her father Dioscorus had been served in 240 A.D. (or it may have been 306 A.D. pedants haggle about it to this day), and allotted a whole lightning bolt to himself.

The sun was setting over the Pacific, and occasionally a ray of golden light peeped through the oil-derricks, as we swung down the last hundred miles into Los Angeles. Louis drove as fast as ever, but I sat happily in my corner, singing loudly the song about the artillery at the Battle of the Marne and how

"... her legend witnesseth
Barbara, the saint of gunners, and a stay in
sudden death!"

and at nightfall we reached the City of the Angels.

Los Angeles is a weird place. I had been warned many times by American friends that I must expect to find a mushroom-town filled to overflowing with exquisitely beautiful young ladies. My first impression was that Los Angeles is a toadstool town filled to over flowing with centenarians. I pottered about the streets in goggling amazement that any place could be so ugly and at the same time contain so many ugly people. Old, old ladies in black billowing skirts and woollen stockings, high boots and ancient hats, clutching in one hand a small carpet-bag and in the other an eighteenth century umbrella, eddied to and fro aimlessly. Old, old gentlemen in suits that must have been dilapidated when Czolgosz shot President McKinley, peered vacantly into shop-windows. The whole population of the town seemed to have completed one century and to have nothing whatever in the world to do except to wait for the completion of a second. I discovered afterwards, of course, that these are the Middle Westerners who have come to Los Angeles to die and find that it is a good deal harder than they expected.

Being citizens of not especially vivid imaginations, they can think of no better occupation than strolling about the streets, thereby giving Los Angeles a worldwide reputation for dowdiness and longevity. The exquisitely beautiful young ladies, on the other hand, do not obtrude themselves on the casual visitor until, he realizes that they are all working in shops, cafés, restaurants, hotels, and so on, holding temporary occupations until such time as they can catch the eye of a Film Director and leap in one bound to Stardom. They are all lovely, and most of them look as if they would steal the blankets off the deathbed of a blind grand-aunt. Many of the accused men and women in the Chicago Police Court looked like innocent little lambkins in comparison with these hard-eyed beauties of Los Angeles.

The toadstool itself is astonishing. Bits of fungoid growth shoot up out of the earth hither and thither. Sometimes it may take the form of a few skyscrapers, sometimes of a garbage-dump, sometimes of a residential quarter, and sometimes of a board announcing that a superlatively big, or luxurious, or beautiful, or all three, building is likely to be put up on that site in the near future, and sometimes of the inevitable mound of rusty cans. The streets are vast and imposing, and often run for miles through the city with nothing on either side except green fields. I should think there is more opportunity for nature-study within the city boundaries of Los Angeles than in any other urban district in the world, and the rabbit shooting must be superb. Indeed, the aged Iowans and Nebraskans must often be reminded of their native prairies when passing down some of the streets of the city of their adoption. The automobiles of Los Angeles provide plenty of amusement for the stranger. There are a great many of them more, I believe, per head of population than in any other town in the world and most of them must have been clanking down the country lanes round the tiny villages of Hollywood and Glendale and Burbank many a long year before the cinematograph industry came to California. The oldest automobiles in the world must be in Los Angeles, coeval, many of them, with the Middle Western veterans. Of course there is a sprinkling of modern automobiles, and here and there a lordly Rolls-Royce glides past with its film star or its bediamonded magnate. But in the main they belong to one or other of those famous categories, the sort that cost fifty dollars ten years ago and the sort that cost ten dollars fifty years ago.

But it is not easy to see much of Los Angeles. Hospitality is so boundlessly lavish, and kindness to visitors so warm and generous, that there is little time for sight-seeing. My chief recollections are a cocktail party in Hollywood of film-actors and actresses, scenarists, playwrights, dialogue writers, and directors, all of whom were British; two days of fog which gave me even more pleasure than the fog at the Berkeley Country Club at San Francisco; the old-world splendour of the porters at the Biltmore Hotel who are dressed as English hunting squires in top-hats, black coats, white breeches, and long boots with orange tops; a visit to the Mexican quarter in the older part of the town; and being compelled to celebrate Armistice Day with a glass of absinthe at ten o clock in the morning. By this time my constitution was having an increasingly difficult struggle with American hospitality, and it was a very jaded traveller who crept surreptitiously out of Los Angeles and escaped in the night to Arizona.

CHAPTER THIRTEEN

Down in Texas the cotton-field, the negro-cabins, drivers
    driving mules or oxen before rude carts, cotton-bales piled
    on banks and wharves. (!)

WALT WHITMAN
My exclamation mark

That night I lay on my green-curtained shelf in the Pullman Car of the Golden State Express — what lovely names they give their big expresses in America! Golden State, Sunset Limited, Black Hawk, Olympian, Flying Texan, Sunshine Special, Texas Ranger, Louisiana Limited, Tomahawk, Copper Country, Dixie Flyer, Flamingo, and many another. I only came across three which puzzled me in this democratic country, and oddly enough, all three were on the same railroad system, the Aristocrat, the Empire Builder, and the American Royal, and only one which was completely out of the tradition of high, sonorous, nomenclature, and that was the Ak-Sar-Ben, which is Nebraska spelt backwards. To resume: that night I lay awake and considered my position with the aid of a map and a thermometer. Taking the map first, I looked at the handful of places I had visited during the course of several months, and the vast area which I had not visited, and the appalling size of the place became more hideously apparent than ever. All the Southern States — a civilization and culture entirely separate from the rest — still remained. The Spanish-French-American uniqueness of New Orleans; the famous city of Charleston; Atlanta, home-town of one of the three greatest golfers the world has ever seen; the Shenandoah Valley and the Valley Pike up which Jackson marched so swiftly and secretly; the battlefields of Fredericksburg and Chancellorsville; Savannah, where Captain Flint, the boozy old sea-man with the blue mug, died of rum; Virginia, the most famous State of all, and the tropical Everglades of Florida, all these were still unvisited and yet they were just part of what I had not seen. Up in the north there were the Appalachians, and the coast of Maine, and Moby Dick's Nantucket, and Yale and Harvard, and — at this point I flung the map away and turned to temperature and pulse. The conclusions were obvious, but I accepted them with reluctance. Firstly, there was what might be called the short-term policy. It consisted of sticking to my Pullman-Car for as long as possible. Only in a Pullman is the European traveller safe from parties. If he once gets out of his haven and stops, if only for a day, in a town which he has never heard of before and of which he is positive that he does not know a single citizen, he is lost. However short he intends to make his visit, however obscure the town may be, so long as it is on the route which his friends know he is going to be taking, then he is doomed. Someone will be on the look-out for him. Some kind host from further back on his voyage will have passed the word to someone in the town to "look out for Mr. So-and-so and be kind to him"; and if Mr. So-and-so puts foot outside the station for so much as an hour he will be nabbed, hustled into an automobile, and within ten minutes he will be listening to the clink of ice in a strong rye-highball that a total but charming stranger will have bought for him.

My only chance, therefore, of avoiding immediate catastrophe was to stick close to my Pullman and go wherever it went, until I felt strong enough to face the world of hosts again.

The second, or Long-Term, policy was arrived at still more reluctantly, for it involved the abandonment of the southern States entirely, with the exception of a long-promised visit to Kentucky. It also meant giving up an excursion which I had planned into Oklahoma, Arkansas, and the Ozark Mountains, and also the coast of Maine. But the map and the thermometer convinced me that I must give up something if I was ever to see the bonnie, bonnie banks of Loch Lomond again, and it was clearly better to put aside the whole of the South for another time, than to rush into it and to rush out again in such a hurry that I would miss everything and yet spoil a second visit by skimming off the cream of first impressions.

I woke up next day in Arizona, and all that day we pounded along a single line of railroad-track down the middle of a wide valley. The scene upon each side of us was identical. Tall, dark yellow grass alternated with patches of sand, the eternal sagebrush — how tired I was getting of sagebrush — alternated with high scrub, and Nature played a dry, hard tune upon the four notes for hours on end. In the distance lay range after range of mountains, their lower slopes blackish green with dense masses of evergreen trees, their summits barren and blue, almost as bright as the mineral blues of the Montana mountains. To me it all looked as useless as the deserts of Utah or Nebraska, but presumably in somebody's eyes it must have found favour, for an interminable wire fence ran on each side of the track. But what the fences were for, whether to prevent non-existent cattle or sheep from straying on to the line, or to dissuade railroad officials from picking bunches of cactus, that stood up everywhere in grotesque shapes, for their sweethearts, I never discovered. To the casual passer-by they certainly appeared to be the most ridiculous fences, built to prevent nothing from straying out of one half of nowhere into the other. But perhaps they meant something to someone.

There were few passengers on that train. I had read all the magazines in the Club-Car at least six times, I had finished all my own books except the Old Testament — and the atmosphere of Los Angeles was still clinging to me sufficiently strongly to put me out of tune with the high moral fervour of Isaiah; looking back on it now, it seems to me that I might have drawn a parallel with my own situation from the story of Lot — and so I sat in the Observation Car and gazed sleepily sometimes at the mountains and sometimes at the twin ribbons of steel that uncoiled themselves so endlessly beneath me, and reflected upon American railroad travel, its comforts and its discomforts. The traveller from Europe, of course, concentrates upon the sleeping arrangements in the Pullman cars when he wants to shoot off a witticism or horrify a circle of maiden-aunts whose only experience of railway locomotion is the annual journey in a "Ladies Only" compartment from London to the seaside, a journey lasting about an hour and a half. The idea of men and women, my dear, all higgledy-piggledy, my dear, and a buck-nigger in charge … and so on.

For some reason this part of American travel never worried me at all. It is true that dressing and undressing is a little awkward, but then I never expect an hotel suite when I board a train in any country. If you want the same luxury as in a British first-class sleeper to Scotland, or in a sleeper of the International Sleeping-Car Company on the Continent of Europe, you can get it in America by paying extra and having a room to yourself. The great mistake is to compare the American Pullman with the European first-class sleeper, instead of with the European night journey spent in a second-class carriage, sitting up all the way, with three travellers on each side. And it is just as well to remember that a berth in an American Pullman for the night costs less than double the compulsory "tip" which you have to give to the conductor on the wagon-lits for service which he does sulkily and badly, and for which the Company ought to pay him.

No, there is a good deal to be said for the Pullman and its slow, courteous, usually venerable African who polishes your shoes, brushes your clothes, and hides your hat in a brown-paper bag. The beds are comfortable, the sheets spotlessly clean, there is always iced water on tap, and the air-conditioning system keeps them at the right temperature and almost entirely free from dust and grime. Then again the American long-distance train is a sort of travelling hotel with its Club Car, its barber shop, its bath, its cocktail-bar, sometimes, its Observation Car, and, for those that want it, its Soda-Fountain. There is usually something to do to pass the time between meals. On the other hand those meals, as a general rule, are unappetizing and very expensive. In fact, if I were ranking the various branches of American cooking which I met during my visit, I would put at the top of the ladder, many rungs above any other, cooking in private homes in Kentucky. Second in the ranking list would be cooking in restaurants in Kentucky, and then, through numerous subtle gradations, we would work down to the last but one, restaurant cooking in New York (outside of Scribe's Club in East Forty-third Street, and André's Restaurant in Frankfort Street), and so to the bottom of the class, Dining-Car cooking on any railroad system.

Drinks, also, when they are obtainable, are very expensive, but as the rules which govern their sale vary with wild capriciousness from one State to another, often the traveller is so pleased and surprised at finding that they are obtainable at all that he pays with little demur the exorbitant price demanded. The Volstead amendment led to some pretty confusion, but the repeal of the Volstead amendment seems to be almost worse. As your transcontinental express runs from State to State, there is an incessant locking and unlocking of the bar in accordance with the local laws, and travellers who have kept a tolerable thirst in check for an hour or two may find that they have in the meantime crossed a fatal border, and that their virtuous self-restraint has gone for less than no reward.

On the credit side of the American railroads must be put the affable, even chatty, politeness of the ticket inspectors, most of whom are dressed in the uniform of an admiral of the fleet, while on the debit side goes the universal absence of a tooth-glass in the washrooms. And finally the beautiful smoothness of the trains on the metals is more than discounted by the fearful jerks and bangs of the stoppings and startings. Whether the engines are not strong enough for the loads they have to pull, or whether the drivers are as inexpert as they seem, a night journey, upon however comfortable a bed, may be made hideous by these jerks at every stopping-place.

After these reflections, I returned to a cow-like inspection of the Arizona scene. We had passed Tucson — almost the only loophole which America has left us through which to reply to their quips about Marjoribanks and Cholmondeley, for it is pronounced Tewson — and there was a little more life in the landscape. Sometimes the dull yellow-brown was enlivened with a splash of genuine green, pale spring-like green, and that always meant water, and water always meant a house and, somewhere or other in that wildness, a wandering cow or two. Once or twice, even, there was a solitary horseman, in blue shirt, ten-gallon hat, and furry trousers, languidly rounding up a few lethargic beasts towards a cattle-pen. The soil grew pink. Palms began to dot the scrub. Short-grass ranges succeeded the long-grass wastes, and on the skyline a row of cactus looked like the trees along a Route Nationale in France after a modern battle has passed that way. The sun sank in kaleidoscopic magnificence over the Arizona mountains, and after dark we entered El Paso, the first town over the Texas border.

As I had an hour to spare I hauled my greatcoat up round my ears, pulled my hat down over my eyes, and went for a stealthy walk. I had a letter of introduction in El Paso and I was taking no chances. However, nothing happened, and I caught, unmolested by would- be hosts with their customary battery of high-balls and old-fashioneds, the night train to Fort Worth.

The less said about that journey across Texas the better. In the first place the sleeping-berths on the Texas and Pacific railroad, after all the kind things I had been thinking about American sleeping-berths in general during the run across Arizona, turned out to be several inches shorter than any I had previously met, and I could not stretch out at full length. Then the engine drivers seemed to be jerkier and joltier than ever, and I lay awake for hours wondering if another of my Wild-West illusions was going to be shattered and if Texas was going to turn out to be a land not of the broad-shouldered giants of my youth, but of little undersized chaps upon whose lack of inches the Texas and Pacific could effect an economy in railroad material. I was also struck from time to time during these dismal watches of the night by the unmistakable smell of oil, which I could not account for.

After a miserable night and an indifferent breakfast, I went to the Observation Car to examine the Texas of Romance, the Texas of the Rangers, of the cattle-trails, of incredible feats with pistol and lasso, of skirmishes with Indians and wild pursuits of Mexicans, of all, in fact, that made life for a child in a London suburb worth living.

But what I saw was a Texas of a thousand oil-derricks, sticking uglily above the horizon, a Texas of pipe-lines running under glorious autumnal leaves, of heavy, oily palls of smoke lowering blackly on to the ranges, of railroad sidings cutting their ways in all directions, crossing and crisscrossing, and twisting and turning, a Texas of square oil-tanks waiting to be filled, of acres of derelict machinery, of huge wheels and shafts and pinions sprawling rustily in golden bushes, of litter and cans and garbage and dirt.

And the climax of the disillusion came when we reached the town of Ranger. Think of it! A town called Ranger in the State of the Texas Rangers. There was Romance for you. But no. Ranger was the most squalid of the lot. It was as if several townlets of the oil country had been picked up, rusty cans, old derricks, smashed automobiles and all, and piled into one enormous dump and labelled Ranger. Even worse than the vast heaps of old iron was the garden suburb, consisting of rows and rows of little wooden houses, each exactly like its neighbours and all of them unoccupied. Nettles sprouted through the windows and saplings grew in the streets. In front of it, facing the railroad, stood a large board on which were painted the words, "Obey Acts ii. 38." I could only assume that those who had built the garden suburb and lived in it, had at least obeyed part of that verse of the Acts of the Apostles, for they certainly had repented.

It was a blessed relief to get out of the oil-country at last into Texas of glorious woods and hillsides that were glowing with orange and crimson. But the damage had been done, and I shall never think happily of Texas again.

Fort Worth and Dallas are an odd pair of neighbours, stuck down side by side on the plains. Fort Worth is old — I walked out to the stone which marks the site of the original Camp Worth of 1839 — Dallas is new. Fort Worth faces west and dreams of the great old days of the past when cattle were the world. Dallas faces east and, very far from dreaming, concentrates eagerly on the great new days of the future when oil and insurance and banking will be the world, and when a century of progress will have made America safe for the middleman and the broker. The streets of Fort Worth are gay with blue shirts and Stetson hats. In Dallas they are sombre with black coats and derby hats. In short, Fort Worth, for all its 120,000 inhabitants, is a village, and Dallas is a cosmopolitan city, and between the two they provide yet another illustration of the unbelievable complexity of the American scene. The more the traveller sees of this continent — for the United States is a continent; it is a cardinal mistake to compare it to this European country or that; it should always be compared to Europe itself — the less he succeeds in understanding it. But there is this consolation. The more he sees of it, the more he ought to understand why he cannot understand it. And after all, if you can see the obstacles in your path, you are halfway to surmounting them.

Take these two towns, Fort Worth and Dallas, and consider how many sidelights upon the social history of America they can throw. They are not very large, they are not very famous, and they are situated in the corner of a State that is a good deal larger than the whole of France. Nevertheless they are a beautiful cross-section of the country. The fort is a memory of the Pioneers, the cattle are symbolical of the first great industry of the South-West. The larger residential houses, hidden in the trees on Lakeside in Dallas, are symbolical of modern prosperity based on modern business, and the skyscrapers, clustered together in bold, if forlorn, imitation of Manhattan, are an example of the herd-instinct run riot. Manhattan is a small island

and so the buildings must climb. Texas is bigger than France and yet the buildings must climb. There is no sense in it, but it is done; and Dallas is much prouder of its lack of sense than it would be if it had planned a beautiful city as Brigham Young's astronomer planned Salt Lake City. The Heraldic Coat of Arms of the United States ought to be a golden skyscraper, alone, on an illimitable field of corn, with the motto, "Well, if Manhattan can do it, why shouldn't we?" It would explain much. Behind the skyscrapers in Dallas there is a quarter of tumble-down, ramshackle wooden houses called Little Mexico. It is full of junk-shops, and small battered warehouses. One café advertises itself as a "tortilla factory," another, the Palace Café, as a "pick-me-up factory." In the children's school at Dallas — and do not forget that Dallas is a Provincial town remote from the eastern and western seaports — there are children of twenty-nine nationalities.

In Fort Worth, overgrown village of spurred and Stetsoned cow-punchers, the bookshop window contained the following books only — about a dozen copies of each — Louisa Alcott's *Little Women*, *Hans Brinker or The Silver Skates*, *Tom Sawyer*, one of the romances of Jules Verne, and *The Swiss Family Robinson*. Dallas, city of hard-faced businessmen, supports four flourishing amateur dramatic societies. The largest of them has a membership of over three thousand, each paying five dollars, and it produces six or seven plays each season, drawing a crowded house for a week with each piece. I saw a list of the plays which this society had performed during the last few years. It might have been the list of the Manchester or Birmingham repertory companies.

There is nothing for it but to shrug the shoulders and give up hope. What can you make of these twin cities of the Texan range one a town of tough cowmen with a taste for fifty-year-old, sentimental stories for schoolgirls, and the other a town of insurance brokers with a passion for the serious drama? What a Continent!

And I did not feel the faintest twinge of surprise — for I had long since been benumbed into a state of mind in which surprise at anything was impossible — when I travelled along the road that links these Texan twins and saw that the only two things of interest on the road were the racecourse on Arlington Downs and a Goldfish Farm.

The huge airport at Dallas was crowded with aeroplanes. In the hangars there were swarms of little biplanes, some painted black and yellow in stripes, like wasps, and some bright scarlet so that they looked like Richthofen's squadron, but on the field itself there were rows of great silver monoplanes, Douglas and Boeing machines, roaring away as their engines were being warmed up for action. They were all private machines, belonging to oil-magnates who were holding a Conference that very morning in Dallas, and they were a great deal more beautiful than their owners, whom I saw later on at luncheon in the hotel.

That luncheon, attended by hundreds of oil-magnates with their attendant sub-magnates, secretaries, advisers, and politicians, put the last nail into the coffin of Texas. Gone forever is my boyhood vision. The derrick has taken the place of the bronco-buster, the legal injunction the place of the six-shooter, and the pasty, flabby-jowled expanse of slab-like countenance of the oil-magnate reigns where once were only lean and sun-tanned faces, blue-eyed, stern, yet with a ready smile.

But even in that exhibition of human codfish lurked something of the American fantasy. That is one of the never-ending charms of the place. You never know when something utterly absurd may not follow instantly on something utterly magnificent, and *vice versa*. Round every corner there may be a Wonder of the World, or a crime, or a rather bad joke, or an ideal, or a dump of rusty cans. You cannot tell which it is going to be. Of only one thing can you be certain, that round every corner you will find something. There is no such thing in America as a complete blank, except perhaps in women's clubs.

Consider the aspect of the American fantasy. You may recall that I had come to Dallas direct from California (and if you do not recall it, you must be the most slipshod reader in existence). Now in California the name of the gentleman who had guaranteed to produce Utopia out of a ballot-box, provided that it was sufficiently full of pro-Utopian votes, had been blazoned on billboards, splashed in newspaper advertisements, placarded on handbills all over the State. In California you could hardly walk fifty yards without seeing his name.

With only the brief interval of that day's transit across Arizona, I had now come to a State where a name was also blazoned on billboards, splashed in newspaper advertisements, placarded on handbills all over the State. In Texas you could hardly walk fifty yards without seeing the name. The name on the Californian billboards stood for the downfall of the Capitalist system. The name on the Texan billboards stood for the triumph of the Capitalist system. The one represented the assault on vested interests, the other represented the apotheosis of vested interests. The one was the spearhead of the attack on Rugged Individualism, the other a shield for the defence. The one cried, "Share the wealth"; the other cried, "Give me the wealth." The one cried, "Give me the power and I'll give you Utopia"; the other thought, "I have the power and so I have Utopia."

And the names were the same. For one was Sinclair, the visionary philosopher; the other was Sinclair, the practical oil-magnate.

CHAPTER FOURTEEN

A Kentucky corn-field, the tall, graceful, long-leav'd corn,
slender, flapping, bright green, with tassels, with
beautiful ears each well-sheath'd in its husk.

WALT WHITMAN

I paid a short — a far too short — visit to Louisville, Kentucky, which I reached by way of Memphis and Nashville. To describe the former would lead me into the trap of trying to describe the Mississippi River, into neither of which I would care to fall, while the outline of the latter is etched by my encyclopaedia with a masterly conciseness that it would be folly to try to emulate. "Nashville is a handsome, well built town, with an imposing capitol of limestone, a penitentiary, and a large lunatic asylum." I travelled across Tennessee, through woods that were denser, higher, and more magnificently gorgeous than any I had yet seen, where the leaves of the ten thousand oak-trees were almost purple in their richness, where few evergreens marred the Cavalier splendour with their Quakerish sobriety, and where no derricks reared their heads, in a train called the Pan American, that modestly describes itself as "One of the World's Most Popular Trains." Whether or not its claim was well founded — I am inclined to doubt the existence of a reliable means of checking it — it certainly was one of the World's Shortest Trains, for it consisted of one coach, one sleeping-car, and one dining-car, and that was all.

My stay in Louisville was the climax of the long whirl round the country. I danced, dined, lunched, played golf, and visited the famous Blue Grass country. The two remarkable things about the Blue Grass are firstly that the grass is green — at least it was when I saw it and secondly that the numerous stud-farms in the district are the proud possessors of no fewer than a hundred and forty — that may not be the exact figure — two-year-olds which are all absolutely certain to win next year's Kentucky Derby. I know, because I saw them all. I also saw the previous winners of about two hundred and sixty

Kentucky Derbys and admired the fluency with which the groom in charge of each hero reeled off its number of victories, the amount of prize money it won during its career down to the nearest nickel, and the list of its most important progeny. The champion of all, a horse called Man of War, had such an imposing figure in the third of these categories that I wanted to ask how he had found the leisure during his career to acquire anything at all in the first two categories, but I refrained. After all, every walk of life has its Eleusinian Mysteries, or, to use a more homely paraphrase, its trade secrets.

But this is not the place to describe the fleeting hours spent among those peaceful green fields, so like England in their freshness and their lanes and their hedgerows, nor the glimpse of home-life in a southern family, as serene and beautiful as the Ohio River which drifted silently along beneath my bedroom window, nor the savour of Kentucky cooking, nor the mellow richness of Kentucky whiskey. It is not even the place to talk of the beauty of the Kentucky ladies whom I had the honour of meeting at a ball in the Pendennis Club. To none of these can justice be done, even remotely, after a wild, whirling visit of four days. For that I must wait till I go back to the South and travel through it from end to end. And may that be soon. Here it must simply be recorded that after four days of southern hospitality and southern laughter and southern gaiety, I departed for New York, leaving behind me a Louisville that was practically a heap of tottering ruins.

CHAPTER FIFTEEN

To get betimes in Boston town I rose this morning early,
Here's a good place at the corner, I must stand and see
    the show.

WALT WHITMAN

It was with a profound diffidence that I approached the city of Boston, partly because of its almost legendary reputation all over the world as the home of a vast Moral Superiority, as the place in which certain old families will only speak to each other, and, higher still, one old family that will only maintain a conversation with Jehovah himself, and partly because a distinguished English author, only a week before my visit, had publicly announced that Boston is a "city of bogus culture." Naturally the Press of the United States had accepted this challenge and splashed the news in great headlines from Coast to Coast, the Bostonian newspapers treating the words with aggrieved protest, the remainder with the whoops of joy that street ragamuffins let loose when they see a top hat dislodged from a dignified and high brow by a snowball. Incidentally these insults, flung about with such lordly abandon by English travellers, do not really assist the work of the English Speaking Union in bringing the United States and Great Britain nearer to each other. A few days' visit, a hasty glance, perhaps a cocktail or two in excess of what the liver will stand, and then a sweeping generalization, and an unpleasant taste is left behind that may take a long time to eradicate.

Fortunately for me, Boston seemed to be standing up pretty well against this ill-tempered attack by one of its guests, and its reprisal was as neat as it was good- humoured. And this was just as well for me, for it was on my head, as the nearest Briton within range, that it fell.

On the first morning of my visit, I was taken in solemn style to see the place beside the old Court-House where the brutal English soldiery shot down in cold blood the unarmed American patriots in 1770. A tablet on the wall marks the spot, and the Lion and the Unicorn, captives of the triumphant Republicans, are compelled by their captors to gaze down for ever from the top of the Court-House on the scene of the Monarchical blunder. Poor Lion and poor Unicorn! They put the best face upon it that they can, and take as much pains to look beautiful as ever they did; but, however dignified they look, however lovely in their mellowed stone, they cannot hide the melancholy fact that there is no crown left to fight for, and that there has been no reason for nearly two hundred years in Boston for the Lion to beat the Unicorn all round the town.

After I had assimilated this page in our annals of Empire I was bundled into an automobile and driven out through New England, past exquisite old Colonial farm-houses and through green fields and quiet woods to the village of Lexington. There, in a little English hamlet, scattered English-wise round an English village-green, stands the monument to the first shots that were fired in the American War of Independence. Rightly does the inscription claim that those shots were heard all round the world, and even for a citizen of the defeated side that village-green is a deeply moving place. On the wall of one little house is a tablet recording that Jonathan Harrington, desperately wounded in the skirmish, struggled thither from the green and died at his wife's feet. From the handful of Jonathan Harrington's companions, from that little patch of grass, from that elm-shaded cluster of white Colonial cottages, came the colossal Republic of which, by weeks and weeks of steady travelling, I had contrived to see a small part, and the echo of those shots did not die away entirely until their sound was lost — it must be for ever — in that other, bigger fusillade, in which the descendants of the English soldiery and of the Lexington farmers stood side by side with the descendants of the men of Lafayette.

From Lexington we went on to Concord, through country of which almost every yard was full of history. Here was a house that had served as the headquarters of an English commander, Earl Percy; yonder, a house at which Paul Revere would unquestionably have halted for a drink, if Paul Revere had chanced to pass that way upon his immortal ride, which unfortunately he omitted to do; and across the fields was the route by which the Royal Troops made their march; and one road to this day is called the Percy Road. And so it was until we came to the little stone bridge in the marshy, reed-filled water-meadows where the brutal English soldiery ran away from the practically unarmed American patriots and so started the ball rolling of the legend that one American farmer with a scythe is worth six English soldiers armed to the teeth with guns and bayonets. I sometimes wonder if the ball has stopped rolling yet. But by this time I was ready to cry "Pax." It seemed as if every turn in the road might bring us to a new monument of British brutality or British humiliation. The landscape seemed, to an imagination that was by now disordered by shame and unhappiness, to be covered with ghostly mercenaries, gross, repulsive, cowardly men, running for their lives from sturdy, honest New England rustics., clear-eyed, clean-limbed, and gallant.

Boston's culture was avenged, and another victory over the Mother Country recorded in the pleasant fields of Massachusetts. I cried "Kamerad," and was allowed time out to visit the graveyard on the hill which looks down upon the village and across to the river and the parsonage where Emerson's father was parson.

I found exactly what I had expected to find — a priceless chapter in America's history being allowed to crumble into dust. The tombstones in historic Concord's graveyard are utterly neglected. The lettering is worn, the stones are covered with gnawing fungus, the grass is growing higher and higher. But nobody cares. In a short hour I collected several perfect examples of eighteenth century funerary inscriptions. Who knows what jewels are still waiting — many of them have got tired of waiting and have joined the shades — for a passer-by who has a taste for such things, a note-book and pencil, and a whole week to spare. Could anything be more lovely, for instance, than this, carved upon a large headstone that stood out by its glittering whiteness among its dingier neighbours?

"This stone is designed by its Durability to perpetuate the memory and by its colour to signify the moral character of Miss Abigail Dudley who died on the fourth of July, 1812, aged 73 years."

Consider also Captain Jonathan Butterick, who was "grave and not double-tongued," and who, when he died in 1757, was "followed to his grave by an aged widow and thirteen well-instructed children."

And was there ever a more perfect tribute paid by a husband to a dead wife than the stone which is sacred to the memory of "Mrs. Rebekah Clark (Comfort of Mr. Benjamin Clark) who died March ye 14th 1788"?

The Christian names of these stern old New England Puritans would make a study in themselves. The best pair which I found in the Concord graveyard were Major Abishai Brown and his wife Jerusha. But in a year or two the stones will have crumbled, and the only memory of Abishai and Jerusha and their daughter Dorcas will be in these pages.

Really the Americans, for all their devastating charm, can be very irritating. There is less excuse here than in sleepy, Spanish Monterey for the callous neglect of the past. Is there not an archaeological society at the mighty

University of Harvard which would make excursions on summer evenings to these forgotten graveyards of New England and copy out the inscriptions and recut the worn lettering just as Walter Scott's Old Mortality used to do? If there is no such archaeological society at Harvard, or among the citizens of Boston itself, then it is high time that one was formed. And if there is neither such a society, nor chance or intention of forming one, then perhaps I suffered unjustly, after all, for the strictures of that distinguished English writer.

It was my intention when composing this book not to mention any of my hosts and hostesses either by name or by identifiable implications, partly because they might not like it, but mainly because there were so many of them and their kindness was so uniformly generous that it would be impossible for sheer lack of space to speak of them all and churlish to speak of some and omit others. So I decided not to speak of any. But in Boston I must break the rule and allow one exception.

I had always been under the impression that, either as an eye-witness at the time, or as a listener, through a long period of subsequent years, I was acquainted with most of the really sensational varieties of escape from sudden death in the World War of 1914-1918. But all were capped, and easily capped, by the escape of my Boston host, Mr. Gardiner Fiske, late of the American Flying Service. Mr. Fiske was observer in a two-seater aeroplane engaged in a mass-combat over the German lines. Noticing that a German aeroplane was about to attack him from behind, he swung his machine-gun round, backwards and upwards, to engage the enemy. Unfortunately the gun came adrift from its moorings and flew out of the cockpit, gun, ammunition-belt, Mr. Fiske and all. Gun and belt dropped to earth. Mr. Fiske flew solitarily through the air and hit the tail of the aeroplane and came to the sudden and discomforting consciousness that he was clinging to the fabric with his hands, with nothing but ten thousand feet of French air between him and French soil. Preferring, therefore, the insubstantial fabric to the very substantial drop, Mr. Fiske hoisted himself, while moving at one hundred and fifty miles per hour, on to the fuselage and then crawled back on all fours along the top of the fuselage and finally dropped head first into his cockpit. It so happened that the observer in the next aeroplane — they were fighting in flight formation — saw the entire episode and, being an amateur artist of distinction, has recorded the whole astounding episode in a series of black-and- white drawings of the various stages of Mr. Fiske's short but stirring odyssey alone and unattached in the upper air.

A curious thing about Boston is the reluctance of the Bostonian to allow the stranger to stroll by himself in the city. Whenever I suggested to any of my friends that I should spend a morning on a solitary ramble, an ominous silence fell and a general awkwardness descended. I never discovered the reason. Perhaps it is an unwritten tradition of Bostonian hospitality that every minute of a guest's day must be filled in for him. Or is it possible that, as in Soviet Russia, there are certain well-established tourist-routes along which a visitor should be courteously but firmly propelled, but beyond the limits of which lurk unnameable horrors? Is it conceivable, I asked myself, as I snatched a couple of minutes from the social whirl and gazed out of my window over the Charles River, is it conceivable that this beautiful old city is a façade behind which voodoo-celebrations, cannibal feasts, medicine-dances, slave-raids, Inquisitionary tortures, and monstrosities of Satanic worship are celebrated in public a few yards from the regular tourist-routes? Somehow I could not believe it. And yet what other explanation was possible of this hermetical sealing, like Mecca, Lhasa, and Timbuctoo, against the foreigner? Why was I not allowed to drift through the streets in search of adventure? It could not be to prevent me from catching a glimpse of that revolting apartment-house which is dressed up to look like a medieval German castle, because I could see it from my window. It could not be that Bostonians have no beautiful buildings to be proud of, for they have hundreds. The problem is at present unsolved. But it is one which ought to be solved in the interests of Sociology, and I commend it, as an exercise in practical research, to those young gentlemen who are studying Sociology at the University of Yale.

But if solitary excursions were banned there were no lack of conducted tours. I visited Harvard and saw the two examples of what a millionaire can do to a University — the Harkness additions, designed to harmonize with the beautiful seventeenth century brick work of the original buildings, and the Widener Library which squats in the middle of it all like a vast, bloated, panting frog with a Greek face.

I went to Fenway Court and saw the Vermeer, one of the supreme pictures of the world, which is placed immediately above a tray of inferior silver ornaments, so that the sunlight reflects the dazzle of the silver on to the surface of the picture, and you find it almost impossible to see the latter and quite impossible to miss the former.

I saw the succession of streets which are named, in the city where Samuel Adams orated and the tea was thrown overboard, after the greatest of England's aristocratic houses, and went round the Museum and inspected the innumerable engravings and paintings of the Church of St. Botolph's in Lincolnshire, the spire of which is Boston Stump, and I came away in the end with two pictures in my mind. One picture was of those, I trust, imaginary scenes of crime and horror that are too hideous for the eye of mortal stranger to rest upon, the other was of quiet, reserved, eighteenth-century squares and streets of residential houses, which, if Bath had been made of dark brick or Boston of creamy stone, might have come straight from that West-English masterpiece of eighteenth century residential architecture. On the whole I preferred the second, or less exciting, of the two pictures.

CHAPTER SIXTEEN

I have offer'd my style to every one, I have journey'd with
    confident step;
While my pleasure is yet at the full I whisper *So long*!"

WALT WHITMAN

The sands were running out. In fact, everything was running out. My time, my store of dollars, my good health, all were rapidly coming to an end when I returned from Boston for one last look round New York before sailing. Those last days were the most difficult of all in many ways. There was so much still to do, so many people still to be seen, so many hosts and hostesses to be thanked for their illimitable kindness. And, on top of all this, the whole of Manhattan Island seemed to be awake to the hideous possibility that a British author was likely to escape from America without delirium tremens, nervous breakdown, cirrhosis of the liver, paralysis of the brain, insomnia, or the staggers. Manhattan sprang to arms with a howl of rage. Such a catastrophe was not to be endured. And, to make the ignominy the more acute, this fearful disaster was likely to occur, not after the usual three or four weeks which is all that is required to get the British author down, but after more than three months. For ninety days and ninety nights, with the exception of a dozen or so spent in the safe obscurity of Pullman cars, the assault had continued unavailingly. Perhaps, thought Manhattan Island, we took it too much for granted. Perhaps we thought that we had so much time at our disposal that the thing was a foregone conclusion. Perhaps we have been half-hearted. Whether that be the case or not, there was nothing half-hearted about the onslaught of those last few days. I was seldom allowed to go to bed at all, and practically the only sleep I got was a few winks in Mr. Isidore Grunbaum's taxi-cab (I hired it and him for the whole period; it saved at least five minutes a day which I would otherwise have spent in getting cabs) while driving from one party to another. It was an epic encounter, and one that deserves a volume to itself, how I fought single-handed against the greatest city of the New World. The result, as you shall see, was in the balance up to the last beating of the gong on the S.S. *Washington*, and the last cries of the stewards warning passengers' friends to go ashore.

One morning I found myself, oddly enough, with a couple of hours to spare. A party had broken up at about seven o clock in the morning, and I was not due at my next engagement until nine o clock, and as I was sauntering homewards and wondering how best to fill in the time, I suddenly remembered that I had a standing invitation to visit the famous Line-Up at the Police Headquarters in Centre Street. A taxi, with a facetious driver who commiserated with me on my unhappy plight, and added that I seemed such a respectable, well-dressed fellow to be in trouble with the cops, and wound up with the philosophic reflection that it was the same old story and that foreign criminals were the curse of the States, deposited me at the grim building, and my card to the Police-lieutenant obtained me instant admission.

It was an illuminating experience in one way, and completely baffling in another. Every foreigner, especially one from Great Britain, ought to be compelled to visit the Line-Up, in order to get the same illumination as I did. Every American ought to be compelled to visit it, in order to get rid of the fundamental cause of the bafflement.

I will try to explain what I mean.

I sat in the auditorium of a large room that is shaped almost like a theatre, among a couple of hundred detectives, and watched the arrested men parade one by one in front of the microphone and under the brilliant limelight. A more dreadful collection of scoundrels I never saw in my life. The prisoners in the Chicago police-court were dregs of humanity because, in the main, their brains were subhuman. They were ape-men whose crimes were almost the crimes of lunatics. But these men in the Centre Street Line-Up were not lunatics. Their brains were not subhuman. Far from it. The bank-robbers, the hold-up men, the machine-gun desperadoes who held in their turn the centre of the stage, were more dangerous than any ape-man. They were clever men turned utterly ruthless, and they looked absolutely terrifying. Although I was surrounded by armed detectives, in the Headquarters of the New York Police, nevertheless it was difficult not to shiver when some of those implacable, deadly eyes happened to turn my way. Their criminal records, so far as they were known, were read out, grim catalogues of cold-blooded murders, of savage beatings, of merciless blackmail, of the kidnapping of babies, of the bombing of harmless tradesmen. They were all young men, and some of them were handsome, like snakes, and almost all were well-dressed. The badly dressed ones were the small fry of crime, pickpockets, sand-baggers and petty larcenists.

Now we come to the point where I got such an eye-opener. At least half of those deadly killers were Italians. Some of them were first generation Italians, men who had been born in Italy, almost always Southern Italy or Sicily, and had come to America during the boom years after the war; and the rest were second or third generation Italians. Next in numbers after the Italians came mixed Slavonic blood, and after them came negroes, then Germans, and finally Americans of the Anglo-Saxon stock.

From this it would appear that when we Europeans talk of American crime and its prevalence, it would be a great deal fairer to talk about European crime in America, or fairer still, European and African crime in America. The post-war slump in Europe caused by the war, and the post-war boom in America caused by the war, combined to attract the cut-throats of the one continent to the throats, so to speak, of the other. And then we get up proudly and say, "What a wicked people the Americans must be compared with us!"

Especially are we fond of making that statement in Great Britain, and especially are we fond of comparing our crime statistics with those of the United States. But the Line-Up convinced me more than ever — not indeed that I wanted any more convincing — that a major cause why Great Britain so often misunderstands the United States, lies in this matter of comparison. The British will insist upon comparing the United States to this country or that, when the only true perspective is to be gained by comparing it to this continent or that. There is no more real sense in saying, "The Americans are more wicked than the British because Italians commit a great many crimes in America," than there would be in saying, "The British are more wicked than the Americans because Italians commit a great many crimes in Naples."

But the moment you compare the United States to Europe, the picture falls into its perspective at once. There is lawlessness in the one just as there is lawlessness in the other, and a murderer may find a hiding-place in the Ozarks as easily as in the Albanian mountains. And it is significant that, whereas John Dillinger appeared in European eyes to be simply another transatlantic desperado in the long succession from the days of the Wild West, to American eyes he was a portent, something of a phenomenon. For Dillinger came of an old-established Anglo-Saxon Quaker family, and was neither dago, wop, nor bohunk, nor of any other imported brand of villainy.

So much for the illumination. Now for the bafflement.

As I watched thug after thug, killer after killer, take his stand in front of us, I could not help feeling that I had seen them all before. And so I had, to all intents and purposes, for they were just the same as the photographs, which I had seen every day in the newspapers or in the post-offices, of notorious criminals. And yet, simply on the strength of these photographs and of the subconscious notion that those men are lineal descendants of Robin Hood, the soft-hearted American public lashes itself into a perfect frenzy of slobbery, weeping sentimentality. The soft-hearted American public does not pause to shed a soft-hearted tear for the old men shot in the stomach by the bandit, or for gallant policemen mown down in a black ambush, or for mothers whose babies are taken and killed by kidnappers. All its soft-heartedness is reserved for the thug. He is regarded as a hero, a figure of romance, and probably as a grand example of Rugged Individualism, and so, by a staggering caprice of inverted reasoning, as an American of whom America ought to be proud. The first sign that a degenerate, dope-maddened, inhuman killer is about to be raised by public opinion pretty nearly to the level of Joan of Arc or St. Francis of Assisi, is when he gets a nickname. Thus Charles Floyd, thief, drug-peddler, bank-robber, and murderer a dozen times over, was christened "Pretty Boy," and a wave of sympathy for the dear charming fellow swept the country. The photograph of "Pretty Boy" lies before me as I write. He was a man of thirty-one (a Belgian by birth, incidentally) with a square face, a broad flat nose, a sulky expression in his narrow eyes, a cruel mouth, and a fat face. But the American public could find something pretty and something boyish in that. In the same way an ugly young murderer with a flabby, pasty face, named George Nelson, is hoisted into a niche beside the heroes of the nation under the name of "Baby-Face." Another newspaper lies before me. It contains the picture of a fat, oily, smartly dressed youth who was serving a life sentence for the murder of two police men in Oklahoma. On Thanksgiving Day he was given six days leave of absence to shoot quail in the mountains. The prison authorities furnished the sweet lad with a shotgun and plenty of cartridges, and then were dreadfully vexed and hurt when he did not return at the end of his six days. So far as I know he has not returned yet, and, at a reasonable estimate, it will cost the lives of five or six brave men before he does. Thug after thug came past on the stage, and my horror deepened as I looked at them. But why, why should the American public sympathize with them? Why is the American public not whole-heartedly on the side of law and order, as the British public is? Our police are no more skilful than the American police, and certainly have not one-twentieth of the difficulties to face nor one-thousandth of the dangers to run, but they get fifty times more successful results. And why? Simply because an overwhelming majority of the citizens is on the side of the police and an enemy of Thugdom.

My mind instinctively went back to the Utah Hotel in Salt Lake City and my young Republican friend with his burning, Crusading zeal and his flood of sincerity and eloquence.... A ruling class ... civic responsibilities ... public servants ... integrity in public life ... Republican duty ... corporate opinion and thence it went to Montana and the memorial to James Williams, the Captain of the Vigilantes, "through whose untiring efforts and intrepid daring Law and Order were established in Montana," and I wondered if the two spirits could not be brought together, the spirit of the Republican Crusaders and the spirit of James Williams, so that a new, continent-wide band of Vigilantes might arise ... untiring ... intrepid ... daring ... to exterminate the murderer and the racketeer, to remove the unjust judge and the paroling Governor, to deal with corruption and graft, just as James Williams and his Vigilantes dealt with men like Sheriff Henry Plummer and George Ives and Buck Stinson and Bob Zackary. It is no business of mine. But all the same, I think the American public ought to be compelled to attend the Line-Up.

A few last engagements remained to be fulfilled before the farewell began, and one of them provided a remarkable experience. A lady had written to me some weeks before, explaining that she was the organizer of a Literary Luncheon, explaining furthermore that a Literary Luncheon consisted of a luncheon — which I had surmised — attended by three or four hundred ladies and gentlemen of immense culture — which I doubted — whose one ambition in life was to listen to a speech by me. After I had declined the invitation, the lady-organizer bombarded me with a perfect *tir de rafale*, or drum-fire, of letters, telephone-calls and telegrams, begging, pleading, cajoling, practically going down on her knees. The Literary Luncheon, it appeared, was steadily becoming frantic with suspense. Indeed, it was pretty clear that, unless I agreed to make a speech to them, not only would the whole Literary Luncheon movement receive a setback that would practically amount to a death-blow, but the individual luncheoners would never fully recover from their chagrin and disappointment. Never before had they looked forward to hearing anyone speak as they were looking forward to hearing me. The date would be a red-letter day in the long and honourable annals of American Culture, and its memory would be for ever enshrined in the hearts of New York's most enlightened citizens. In this lyrical strain the lady-organizer couched her appeals, and in the end I cancelled a very attractive engagement and agreed to deliver a harangue. A loud paean of thanksgiving instantly rocked the welkin in Literary and Lunching circles when the news got round, and the jubilation was, according to the lady-organizer, so unparalleled that I took a good deal of trouble over the preparation of my speech. I felt that it was the least I could do.

There were about three hundred people in the room. The steam-heating was in full blast and the room was very stuffy. The food was execrable. There was nothing to drink. And when I arrived the lady-organizer (who reminded me very strongly of Miss E. M. Delafield's delicious creation, Miss Katherine Ellen Blatt, in her *Provincial Lady in America*) informed me with perfect sang-froid, with the blandest nonchalance, and without the faintest batting of an eyelid, that the principal speaker was dear Mr. Beverley Nichols, that I was sixth speaker on the list, and would I be kind enough to condense what I had to say into an absolute limit of four minutes, and of course if I could make it shorter so much the better. In the end I was relegated to seventh place as the speaker who was scheduled for Number Seven was rather important and was in a hurry to get away and so was promoted in the list. My turn came on at a quarter past three and the hot-house, in which we were by this time gasping, was rapidly emptying. I spoke for two minutes and twenty-five seconds and the lady-organizer interrupted me four times.

Life is full of ups and downs, especially in the United States. Within a few hours I had almost forgotten the villainous Literary Luncheon and was basking in the conversation of Mr. Christopher Morley. We strolled at our ease through Manhattan and loafed across Brooklyn Bridge to look at the house in which *Leaves of Grass* first saw the light. I need hardly add, at this stage of this book, that this historical monument of one of America's greatest writers is utterly neglected. It is true that there is a bronze tablet — of singular ugliness — on the wall in commemoration of the building's great distinction, but there is no attempt to preserve the structure. When I saw it, the house was disused, and boards were nailed across the cobwebby windows. By this time it may have vanished altogether. Thence we wandered back over the bridge and called on Mr. Isaac Mendoza, most delightful of booksellers, bearing the wisdom of his seventy years under an exterior of about forty, and talked for hours in his narrow-fronted little bookshop in Ann Street, and then the three of us dined at André's restaurant in Frankfort Street where the Oyster Pot Pie almost brings tears of emotion to the eyes, and every menu begins with the immortal words, "*Le vin dissipe la tristesse et réjouit le cœur*," and Literary Luncheons and lady-organizers fade into nothingness.

Mr. Morley and I pursued our Whitman pilgrimage out to Long Island on the next day and visited the little farmhouse where he was born. By some odd chance, the farmhouse is not tumbling down into ruin. On the other hand there is no commemorative tablet nor any other outward sign of its historic interest. Perhaps American public opinion feels that by not actually destroying the birthplace of the poet it has done enough for posterity. This is the last reference which I shall make to the American enigma. But it ought to be placed on record that if each citizen of the United States who, during my visit to their country, made some reference in conversation with me to the deplorable lack of historical antiquities in America, were to contribute the sum of one dollar for each reference, a fund would be raised that would be sufficient to save the Walt Whitman house at the end of Brooklyn Bridge, to save the General Castro house and the Spanish Bear-Pit at Monterey, to remove the stucco renovations from the oldest house in San Francisco, to recut the tombstones in the graveyards of the Trinity Church at the end of Wall Street and in Concord, Massachusetts, to destroy the pre-fire water-tower in Chicago, to repair the crumbling roof of the Church of the Mission of San Miguel Arcangel, and that there would still be enough left over to finance the removal of the Elevated from Third Avenue.

The winds of winter were screaming icily round our ears as we came back from the Whitman house, past Louis Quinze châteaux and Louis Quatorze châteaux, and, here and there, a strikingly original departure in the form of a Louis Treize château, past the aviation field from which Colonel Lindbergh took off for his flight to Europe, in the days when he was not a world-hero but just a Lone Fool. And, incidentally, if the fund for the removal of the Elevated from Third Avenue was increased by a dollar from each American man, woman, and child who honestly believe that Colonel Lindbergh was the first airman to fly the Atlantic, it would be large enough to pay off the National Debt. At Roslyn, we stopped at the Post Office and Mr. Morley showed me a bulletin from the Department of Justice appealing for help in tracking down a murderous desperado named Robert Mais. The usual photograph and description was supplemented by an extra piece of information that must have been of great help to amateur trackers. For Mr. Mais had been indiscreet enough, in earlier life, to have his right forearm tattooed with a Heart pierced by an Arrow, with the single word over it "Mother," and the Department of Justice appealed to every right-minded citizen to report to the police the whereabouts of any murderer that was thus adorned. As I opened my newspaper next morning at breakfast, two photographs shot out at me simultaneously. The first announced that Mr. Henry Ford was contemplating the demolition, transportation to America, and subsequent re-erection, of Bull's Cottage, in Boreham, Essex, the cottage in which Ann Boleyn lived while Henry VIII was courting her in the early fifteen hundreds. Mr. Ford had bought the whole Boreham estate, and presumably felt that one Henry ought to get his money's worth as well as another. The second paragraph announced the imminent destruction, with out re-erection, of the colonial Fountain House on Staten Island that was at one time the headquarters of the British army during the War of Independence, and the house of Margaret Moncrieffe, who was in love with Aaron Burr.

I made one last dash out of New York City, to the town of Paterson, New Jersey.

It is a manufacturing town, full of silk-factories, and Italian strikers, and Jews working away in little side-streets and undercutting prices, and small, shabby houses, and a jostling, crowded Main Street. But there was one beautiful thing I saw in the "Lyons of America" the like of which I saw nowhere else, and that was the Falls of the Passaic River, almost in the middle of the town, frozen hard and glittering in the afternoon sun of winter with a sort of creamy colour where the foam had been struck into stillness by the frost. It was as if Nature had said, with a sardonic wink, "See what I can do with my Falls in the night. All you can do with them in a century is to make Paterson."

I did my round of farewells and slipped unostentatiously down to the Quay.

I was still alive and that was more than I had any right to expect. But one more party, I felt, might just be the one more which would snatch victory for the United States out of the jaws of defeat. One more party, and I would be laid to rest in one of those open spaces in Queens.

So I crept down to the steamship *Washington* without a word to a soul, and tiptoed silently to my cabin. Once inside my cabin, with the door locked and bolted, I should be safe. I reached it unobserved and darted in. It was full of friends who had come to see me off, and a bottle was whizzing round from hand to hand.

But there is an end to everything and the liner left at last. I went up to the deck and looked back at Manhattan. Far in the distance the spidery lines of the George Washington Bridge were faintly visible in the haze, and the Downtown skyscrapers shone in the bright wintry sun, each wearing its white panache of steam. The giant steamships lay snugly in their berths and the little boats of the Squeedunk Railroad bustled importantly past. The gulls cried round us and the enchanted outline faded.

That night I could not sleep. A strong wind had arisen, and I stood for hours in the darkness on the sun-deck, and listened to the wind and the rush of water round the bows of the liner, and looked out across the seas and thought of all I had seen and done in America. And most of all I thought of the friends I had made, friends that I know I will never lose, and of the gay and happy people I had seen, and of the immensity of America, and of the unquenchable spirit of the Pioneers that still lives on and always will live on.

And I thought of the sun shining upon Chesapeake Bay, and of the blueness of the mountains of Montana, and of the cottonwoods on the Elkhorn River, and of the crusading fire of the Young Republicans, and of the yellow elm-leaves drifting slowly down in Liberty Park in Salt Lake City, and of the Carroll House, and of the village-green at Lexington, and of Monterey, and of the steamer for Rarotonga going out through the Golden Gate into the Pacific.

THE END